LEONARDO DA VINCI · THE ARTIST
BY LUDWIG GOLDSCHEIDER
PUBLISHED BY THE PHAIDON PRESS

* DRAPERY STUDY.   WINDSOR CASTLE, ROYAL LIBRARY (See note 36-A)

LEONARDO DA VINCI

LONDON · PHAIDON PRESS

NEW YORK · OXFORD UNIVERSITY PRESS

PUBLISHED BY THE PHAIDON PRESS · 1944 · 41 MUSEUM STREET · LONDON
AND 14 ST. GILES · OXFORD

SECOND EDITION

MADE IN GREAT BRITAIN
PRINTED BY CLARKE & SHERWELL LTD · LONDON AND NORTHAMPTON

FOREWORD

THE PRESENT WORK is not a book on Leonardo. It is rather a book by him.

It contains large-scale reproductions of all his paintings, together with some which are reasonably ascribed to him. It also reproduces some sculptures, thought to be his. But the best part of the book concerns Leonardo's drawings, most of which are given in their original size. *6606*

Besides the actual reproductions of Leonardo's work, there is his biography by Vasari, who was a boy of eight when Leonardo died. There is also a number of documents—letters by Leonardo and information by his contemporaries, which combine to show how Leonardo's work appeared to those who lived and worked with him. A systematic bibliography and some notes on the plates will help readers to find their way through the maze of Leonardo discussions, if they are eager or curious enough to wander so far.

Actually, the plates, the documents, the master's biography by Vasari, and the passages from other biographies, enable everyone to make up his own book on Leonardo by reading this one. He will see what Leonardo did, he can study information directly from the Master and from his contemporaries—and he probably does not want more.

It was not originally my intention to put anything of my own into this book, but I have found it necessary to include here several hundred notes, to make the reader acquainted with modern judgments on Leonardo. For fuller information the reader is referred to the books mentioned in the bibliography, but in these notes I could not help saying a few things that are new. Thus, for instance, I have ventured an explanation of the "knots", I have attempted to identify the "Profile drawing of a Man" at Windsor, I have given a hint regarding the Self-Portrait. I fancy I have found something which might facilitate research into the lost portrait of Amerigo Vespucci. I have read, for the first time, the inscription on the Pacioli portrait. I have commented upon the two words on the scroll of the Ambrosiana Musician. I have invited the reader to consider a new theory of Leonardo as the restorer of the " Nile". Many similar things may be found by an inquirer in the captions and in the comparative illustrations.

Since my early share in editing a book on Leonardo, I have seen most of Leonardo's work again. First, I happened to live in the city where Leonardo's most beautiful female portrait is housed, the portrait of Ginevra, the Lady of the Juniper. Then I saw again the two paintings in Florence and Rome, which are called unfinished, but which indeed belong to the world's most perfect works of art—" a work of art is finished when an artist achieves his aim," to quote Rembrandt. Shortly after, when homeless in Paris, I found just enough time to see once more the Mona Lisa and the St Anne. But the other St Anne, the one in London, is a picture I shall never forget   I can always see it distinctly whenever I close my eyes. It is a disquieting and heart-confusing work, like a poem by Sappho, a vision in the twilight. The Nymph, in a drawing at Windsor, pointing into the distance beyond the stream, fills us with the same mood. When shall we see all that again ?

My thanks are due to many people who helped me : to Irma A. Richter, who gave me permission to quote from Jean Paul Richter's second edition of Leonardo's Literary Works (Oxford University Press, 1939) ; to the publishers, Messrs. J. M. Dent & Son, Ltd., of the Everyman Library for permission to use Mr. A. B. Hinds' translation of Vasari ; to Sir Kenneth Clark, who kindly gave his criticism on the plates before they were printed ; to Mr. W. G. Meredith, one of the pioneers of photogravure printing in England, who lent his experience of thirty years to the work of reproducing these plates ; to Philip Hendy for friendly advice ; to Prefetto G. Galbiati, of the Milan Ambrosiana ; to Mr. O. F. Morshead, of the Royal Library at Windsor Castle, and to Mr. A. E. Popham, of the British Museum, who assisted me with photographs ; and I am lastly grateful to the curators and owners of many collections for assistance in procuring new photographs and for information imparted to me in conversation and by letter.

London, 1943   LUDWIG GOLDSCHEIDER

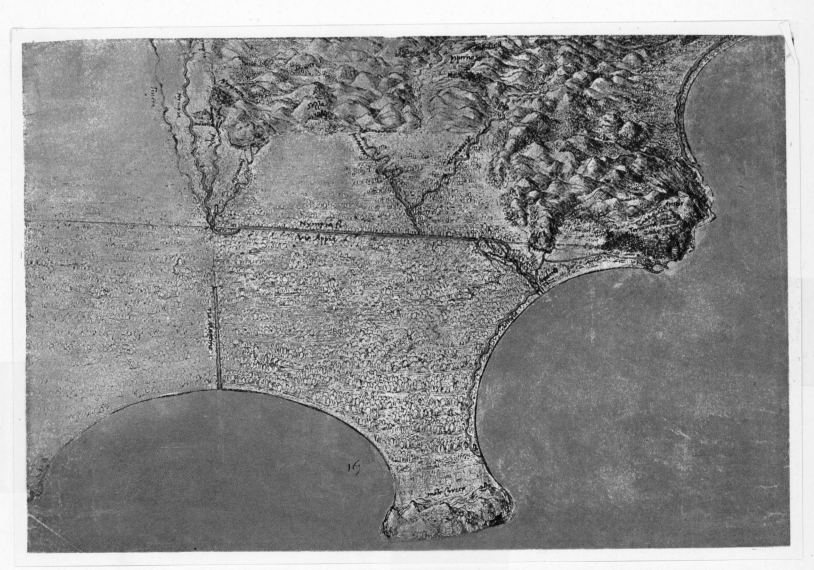

Fig. 1. Leonardo: Map of the coast south of Rome, crossed by the Via Appia. Pen and Ink, and blue watercolour ; c. 1514. Windsor Castle, Royal Library (No. 12684).

LIFE OF LEONARDO DA VINCI
PAINTER AND SCULPTOR OF FLORENCE
BY GIORGIO VASARI · 1568

THE heavens often rain down the richest gifts on human beings naturally, but sometimes with lavish abundance bestow upon a single individual beauty, grace and ability, so that, whatever he does, every action is so divine that he distances all other men, and clearly displays how his genius is the gift of God and not an acquirement of human art. Men saw this in Leonardo da Vinci, whose personal beauty could not be exaggerated, whose every movement was grace itself and whose abilities were so extraordinary that he could readily solve every difficulty. He possessed great personal strength, combined with dexterity, and a spirit and courage invariably royal and magnanimous, and the fame of his name so spread abroad that, not only was he valued in his own day, but his renown has greatly increased since his death.

This marvellous and divine Leonardo was the son of Piero da Vinci.(1) He would have made great profit in learning had he not been so capricious and fickle, for he began to learn many things

---

(1) *The little town of Vinci is situated in Tuscany between Empoli and Pistoja, about 60 miles from Florence. Vasari calls Leonardo's father "Ser" Piero, a title borne by notaries. Ser Piero was engaged from 1451 onwards in his profession, mainly in Florence, where he became one of the most sought-after notaries. Leonardo, the illegitimate son of Ser Piero and the peasant maid, Catarina, was born in 1452 at Anchiano, a village near Vinci. The year of Leonardo's birth was not known until the 18th century, when it was authenticated through the publication of an assessment of property belonging to his grandfather, dated 1457. Vasari did not know it.*

Fig. 2. Portrait of Verrocchio, by Lorenzo di Credi, c. 1485. Florence, Uffizi. *Leonardo was Verrocchio's pupil ; but his favourite disciple and the executor of his will was Lorenzo di Credi, who finished for him the Pistoja altar-piece and other works.*

Fig. 3. Portrait of Leonardo. Woodcut from Vasari, *Le Vite,* 1568

and then gave them up.(2) Thus in arithmetic, during the few months that he studied it, he made such progress that he frequently confounded his master by continually raising doubts and difficulties.(3) He devoted some time to music, and soon learned to play the lyre, and, being filled with a lofty and delicate spirit, he could sing and improvise divinely with it.(4) Yet though he studied so many

---

(2) *Paolo Giovio, in his short biography of Leonardo, dated about 1530, judged similarly but more comprehendingly ; after mentioning Leonardo's exertions "in the sciences and the liberal arts," his optical and anatomical studies, he adds regretfully: "But while he was thus spending his time in the close investigation of subordinate branches of his art he brought but very few works to completion, for his masterly facility and his fastidious disposition caused him to discard many works he had already begun."*

(3) *McCurdy assumes that Leonardo's teacher in mathematics was Benedetto dell'Abbaco, the most famous man of his calling in Florence. Leonardo, moreover, continued to cultivate the study of mathematics all his life, and about 1497 collaborated in* Divina Proportione, *the work of his friend, Fra Luca Pacioli ; the geometrical figures in the 1509 edition are after Leonardo's drawings. Mathematics was for him the foundation of art, and on the back of a drawing (Windsor 19118) he wrote : "Let no man who is no mathematician read the elements of my work."*

(4) *Paolo Giovio, Anonimo Gaddiano, Luca Pacioli and Lomazzo, all mention Leonardo's musical talent, a gift which he shared with Piero della Francesca, Giorgione, and his teacher Verrocchio. Paolo Giovio relates : "He sang beautifully to his own accompaniment on the lyre to the delight of the entire Court."*

different things, he never neglected design and working in relief, those being the things which appealed to his fancy more than any other. When Ser Piero perceived this, and knowing the boy's soaring spirit, he one day took some of his drawings to Andrea del Verrocchio,(5) who was his close friend, and asked his opinion whether Leonardo would do anything by studying design. Andrea was so amazed at these early efforts that he advised Ser Piero to have the boy taught. So it was decided that Leonardo should go to Andrea's workshop.(6)   The boy was greatly delighted, and not only practised his profession, but all those in which design has a part. Possessed of a divine and marvellous intellect, and being an excellent geometrician, he not only worked in sculpture, doing out of clay some heads of women smiling, which were reproduced in gypsum, and children's heads also, executed like a master,(7) but also prepared many architectural plans and elevations, and he was the first, though so young, to propose to canalize the Arno from Pisa to Florence.(8)   He made designs for mills, fulling machines, and other engines to go by water, and as painting was to be his profession he studied drawing from life. He would make clay models of figures, draping them with soft rags dipped in plaster, and would then draw them patiently on thin sheets of cambric or linen, in black and white, with the point of the brush.(9)   He did these admirably, as may be seen by specimens in my book of designs. He also drew upon paper so carefully and well that no one has ever equalled him. I have a head in grisaille which is divine. The grace of God so possessed his mind, his memory and intellect formed such a mighty union, and he could so clearly express his ideas in discourse, that he was able to confound the boldest opponents. Every day he made models and designs for the removal of mountains with ease and to

Fig. 4. Leonardo : Drapery study in black and white on cambric linen, c. 1472. Florence, Uffizi.

pierce them to pass from one place to another, and by means of levers, cranes and winches to raise and draw heavy weights; he devised a method for cleansing ports, and to raise water from great depths, schemes which his brain never ceased to evolve. Many designs for these notions are scattered about, and I have seen numbers of them. He spent much time in making a regular design of a series of knots so that the cord may be traced from one end to the other, the whole filling a round space. There is a fine engraving of this most difficult design, and in the middle are the words : *Leonardus Vinci Academia.*(10)   Among these models and designs there was one which he several times showed to many able citizens who then ruled Florence, of a method of raising the church of San Giovanni and putting steps under it without its falling down. He argued with so much eloquence that it was not until after his departure that they recognized the impossibility of such a feat.

His charming conversation won all hearts, and although he possessed nothing and worked little, he kept servants and horses of which he was very fond, and indeed he loved all animals, and trained them with great kindness and patience. Often, when passing

---

(5) *Andrea di Michele de' Cione, called Verrocchio ("True-Eye"), born in Florence 1435, died in Venice 1488 ; pupil of the goldsmith Giuliano Verrocchio and of Donatello. Best known through his bronze equestrian statue of Colleoni in Venice, which was not completed by him (but by A. Leopardi, 1496) and not set up until after the Master's death.*

(6) *It is uncertain in which year Leonardo entered Verrocchio's Bottega (workshop). Most of the authorities (including Müller-Walde, Thiis, Hildebrandt, Maclagan and van Marle) assume this to be 1466, but others (Ravaisson-Mollien, Richter, Venturi, and de Rinaldis) believe this event did not take place until 1470. As Leonardo was a member of the Florence Guild of Painters in 1472, as transpires from an entry in "the red book of Debtors and Creditors of the Company of the Painters," the assumption that he was taken into Verrocchio's workshop about four years before, i.e., when he was sixteen, in 1468, is the most probable. On the 1st January, 1478, Leonardo received his first independent commission ; in March, 1481, the contract for the "Adoration of the Kings" was entered into, and at this time Leonardo was working in his own dwelling, and no longer with Verrocchio. By July, 1481, the model for the equestrian statue of Colleoni was finished in Verrocchio's workshop in Florence, and thereafter Verrocchio lived permanently in Venice. A short time afterwards (1482) Leonardo removed to Milan. His connection with Verrocchio had lasted about fifteen years.*

(7) *Lomazzo (Treatise on Painting, Milan 1584, p. 127) mentions a terracotta head of the infant Christ in his collection, "by Leonardo's own hand" ; also a clay relief of a horse by Leonardo, in the collection of the sculptor Leone Leoni. All these sculptural works of Leonardo's youth are lost, and all we know for certain about Leonardo as a sculptor is based on a few drawings ; all the attributions are mere conjectures (cf. plates 147-150).*

(8) *The aim of the plan was to procure for Florence direct access to the sea. Numerous drawings connected with this idea have been preserved. (Cf. e.g. Richter §§ 1001, 1006; Clark, Nos. 12279, 12659.) Leonardo was particularly occupied with this idea in the summer of the year 1503. (See G. B. Venturi, Essai sur les ouvrages physico-mathemat. de L. da V., Paris 1797, p. 39.)*

(9) *A good and richly illustrated survey of these drapery drawings, which were executed in Verrocchio's studio for study purposes, is to be found in Bernhard Berenson's "The Drawings of the Florentine Painters", amplified edition, Chicago 1938 ; particularly figs. 517-531. One of the three drapery drawings painted on canvas in the Uffizi is reproduced here (fig. 4). Similar drawings may be seen in the Louvre and in the British Museum. How such drawings were employed in painting is shown by fig. 6. Drapery drawings from clay models were, in the earlier Renaissance, rather usual, and not in Verrocchio's workshop alone. In the life of Piero della Francesca (about 1416-1492), Vasari says : "Piero was in the habit of making clay models, covering them with soft cloth with a number of folds in order to copy them and turn them into account." In the Life of Lorenzo di Credi Vasari speaks of "drawings copying clay models draped in waxed cloth". (Cf. pl. 37.)*

(10) *Six of these engravings have been preserved. Albrecht Dürer copied them (Richter, I. p. 387. n.). From the inscription on these knots (fig. 5) it has been assumed that Leonardo was the director of a drawing academy (school) in Milan, but this supposition is now generally discredited. I should like to put forward the suggestion that these engravings represent tickets for scientific disputations, being either tickets of admission or prize tickets. By "academia" was understood in the Renaissance a poetical or scientific tourney ; "academia coronaria" was the name of the poetical competition which Leon Battista Alberti organized in the Florence Cathedral on the 22nd October, 1441. But why was a knot used as an emblem for Leonardo's "Academia", and what is the reason for the interlacing ornaments on the dress of Mona Lisa and in other paintings? The explanation is a play on the words vincire (to fetter, to lace, to knot) and Vinci ; being a cryptographic signature of Leonardo da Vinci. The interlaced pattern was, however, not invented by Leonardo, but was known since the days of the Celts (e.g. the "Domnach Airgid", c. 1000 A.D.).*

Fig. 5. School of Leonardo : Knot, engraving. c. 1510. London, British Museum.
This "fantasia dei vinci", a pattern of linked chains, is most probably a hieroglyphic signature of Leonardo.

Fig. 6. Detail from Verrocchio's Baptism, c. 1482. Florence, Uffizi (cf. fig. 7).
The angel on the left painted by Leonardo.

places where birds were sold, he would let them out of their cages and pay the vendor the price asked. Nature had favoured him so greatly that in whatever his brain or mind took up he displayed unrivalled harmony, vigour, vivacity, excellence, beauty and grace. His knowledge of art, indeed, prevented him from finishing many things which he had begun, for he felt that his hand would be unable to realize the perfect creations of his imagination, as his mind formed such difficult, subtle and marvellous conceptions that his hands, skilful as they were, could never have expressed them. His interests were so numerous that his inquiries into natural phenomena led him to study the properties of herbs and to observe the movements of the heavens, the moon's orbit and the progress of the sun.

Leonardo was placed, as I have said, with Andrea del Verrocchio in his childhood by Ser Piero, and his master happened to be painting a picture of St John baptising Christ. For this Leonardo did an angel holding some clothes, and, although quite young, he made it far better than the figures of Andrea.(11) The latter would never afterwards touch colours, chagrined that a child should know more than he. Leonardo was next employed to draw a cartoon of the Fall of Man, or Adam and Eve, for a portière in tapestry, to be made in Flanders of gold and silk, to send to the King of Portugal.(12) Here he did a meadow in grisaille, with the lights in white lead, containing much vegetation and some animals, unsurpassable for finish and naturalness. There is a fig-tree, the leaves and branches beautifully foreshortened and executed with such care that the mind is amazed at the amount of patience displayed. There is also a palm-tree, the rotundity of the dates being executed with great and marvellous art, due to the patience and ingenuity of Leonardo. This work was not carried farther, and the cartoon is now in Florence in the fortunate house of Ottaviano de' Medici the Magnificent, to whom it was given not long ago by Leonardo's uncle.(13)

It is said that when Ser Piero was at his country-seat he was requested by a peasant of his estate to get a round piece of wood painted for him at Florence, which he had cut from a fig-tree on his farm. Piero readily consented, as the man was very skilful in catching birds and fishing, and was very useful to him in such matters. Accordingly Piero brought the wood to Florence and asked Leonardo to paint something upon it, without telling him its history. Leonardo, on taking it up to examine it one day, found it warped, badly prepared and rude, but with the help of fire he made it straight, and giving it to a turner, had it rendered soft and smooth instead of being rough and rude. Then, after preparing the surface in his own way, he began to cast about what he should paint on it, and resolved to do the Medusa head to terrify all beholders. To a room, to which he alone had access, Leonardo took lizards, newts, maggots, snakes, butterflies, locusts, bats, and other animals of the kind, out of which he composed a horrible and terrible monster, of poisonous breath, issuing from a dark and broken rock, belching poison from its open throat, fire from its eyes, and smoke from its nostrils, of truly terrible and horrible aspect. He was so engrossed with the work that he did not notice the terrible stench of the dead animals, being absorbed in his love for art. His father and the peasant no longer asked for the work, and when it was finished Leonardo told his father to send for it when he pleased, as he had done his part. Accordingly Ser Piero went to his rooms one morning to fetch it. When he knocked at the door Leonardo opened it and told him to wait a little, and, returning to his room, put the round panel in the light on his easel, and having arranged the window to make the light dim, he called his father in. Ser Piero, taken unaware, started back, not thinking of the round piece of wood, or that the face which he saw was painted, and was beating a retreat when Leonardo detained him and said, "This work has served its purpose ; take it away, then, as it has produced the effect intended." Ser Piero indeed thought

(11) *Albertini's description of Florence, 1510, already mentions Leonardo's share in this painting (The angel on the left, see figs. 6 and 7). Not only the Angel, but also the Landscape and probably also the body of Christ have been painted over by Leonardo, and indeed with oil colours above Verrocchio's tempera. (Bode, Leonardo-Studien, 1921, pp. 10-14.) The tuft of grass beside the kneeling angel testifies to the same understanding of the life of plants as Leonardo's later plant studies (cf. e.g. plate 114).*

(12) *This cartoon has disappeared. Suida surmises that Raphael's "Fall of Man" in the Stanza della Segnatura of the Vatican is a free rendering of Leonardo's lost cartoon.*

(13) *Francesco, a brother of Leonardo's father. He dwelt, probably as a countryman and silk-worm rearer, in Vinci, and died in 1506 or 1507. But Allessandro degli Amadori, a brother of Ser Piero's first wife, also called himself Leonardo's uncle ; in 1506 he interpreted to Leonardo the wishes of Isabella d'Este. (Beltrami, Documenti, Nos. 173, 174.) I believe that Messer Allessandro Amadori, Canonico di Fiesole, was the first owner of Leonardo's "Fall of Man".*

Fig. 7. Verrocchio: Baptism of Christ, begun c. 1475. Florence, Uffizi.
Painted in tempera, overpainted in oil by Leonardo.

Fig. 8. Leonardo: The Angel of Annunciation, pen and sepia drawing (part), c. 1506.
Windsor Castle, Royal Library (No. 12328).

it more than miraculous, and he warmly praised Leonardo's idea. He then quietly went and bought another round wheel with a heart transfixed by a dart painted upon it, and gave it to the peasant, who was grateful to Piero all his life. Piero took Leonardo's work secretly to Florence and sold it to some merchants for one hundred ducats, and in a short time it came into the hands of the Duke of Milan, who bought it of them for three hundred ducats.(14)

Leonardo next did a very excellent Madonna, which afterwards belonged to Pope Clement VII. Among other things it contained a bowl of water with some marvellous flowers, the dew upon them seeming actually to be there, so that they looked more real than reality itself.(15) For his good friend Antonio Segni he drew a Neptune on paper, with so much design and care that he seemed alive.(16) The sea is troubled and his car is drawn by sea-horses, with the sprites, monsters, and south winds and other fine marine creatures. The drawing was given by Antonio's son Fabio to Messer Giovanni Gaddi with this epigram:

Pinxit Virgilius Neptunum, pinxit Homerus,
Dum maris undisoni per vada flectit equos.
Mente quidem vates illum conspexit uterque,
Vincius ast oculis ; jureque vincit eos.(17)

Leonardo then had the fancy to paint a picture of the Medusa's head in oils with a garland of snakes about it, the most extraordinary idea imaginable, but as the work required time, it remained unfinished, the fate of nearly all his projects.(18) This is among the treasures in the palace of Duke Cosimo, together with the head of an angel, who is raising an arm in the air, this arm being foreshortened from the shoulder to the elbow, while the other rests

(14) *Now lost.*
(15) *Cf. note to plate 68.*
(16) *For a study to this lost drawing see plate 57.*
(17) *The meaning of this Latin epigram is roughly as follows. "Virgil and Homer both depicted Neptune driving his sea-horses through the rushing waves. The poets saw him in their imaginations, but Leonardo with his own eyes, and so he rightly surpassed them." There is a pun on the words* Vincius (*the man from* Vinci) *and* vincit (*he vanquished*) *which is untranslatable.*
(18) *Lost. The panel in the Uffizi at Florence, which was once erroneously supposed to be Leonardo's Head of the Medusa, is a work of the 17th century, and actually an adaptation of the head on a shield in the "Struggle for the Standard" (cf. fig. 18). But it may be that "The Head of the Medusa" by Rubens in the Vienna Gallery is a free version of Leonardo's lost painting.*
(19) *Cf. the note to plate 100 and fig. 8.*

on its breast.(19) So marvellous was Leonardo's mind that, desiring to throw his things into greater relief, he endeavoured to obtain greater depths of shadow, and sought the deepest blacks in order to render the lights clearer by contrast. He succeeded so

Fig. 9. Leonardo: Scaramuccia, black chalk drawing, c. 1508.
Oxford, Ashmolean Museum.

Fig. 10. Portrait of Amerigo Vespucci, by an unknown Florentine Painter (copy after Leonardo?). Florence, Uffizi.

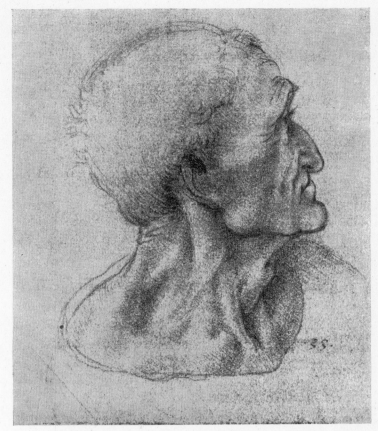

Fig. 11. Leonardo: Study for the Judas in the Last Supper, red chalk on red paper, c. 1495. Windsor Castle, Royal Library (No. 12547).

well that his scenes looked rather like representations of the night, there being no bright light, than of the lightness of day, though all was done with the idea of throwing things into greater relief and to find the end and perfection of art.

Leonardo was so delighted when he saw curious heads, whether bearded or hairy, that he would follow about anyone who had thus attracted his attention for a whole day, acquiring such a clear idea of him that when he went home he would draw the head as well as if the man had been present. In this way many heads of men and women came to be drawn, and I have several such pen-and-ink drawings in my book, so often referred to. Among them is the head of Amerigo Vespucci,(20) a fine old man, drawn in carbon, and that of Scaramuccia, the gipsy captain, which afterwards belonged to Messer Donato Valdambrini of Arezzo, canon of San Lorenzo, left to him by Giambullari.(21) He began a picture of the Adoration of the Magi, containing many beautiful things, especially heads, which was in the house of Amerigo Benci, opposite the loggia of the Peruzzi, but which was left unfinished like his other things.(22)

On the death of Giovan Galeazzo, Duke of Milan, and the accession of Ludovico Sforza in the same year, 1494,(23) Leonardo was invited to Milan with great ceremony by the duke to play

(20) *In the Uffizi there is a portrait of Amerigo Vespucci as an old man (fig. 10). This portrait bears such resemblances to some of the heads in Leonardo's "Adoration of the Kings", the "St Jerome", and especially the Windsor drawing of Judas (fig. 11) that the unknown painter of this portrait might be presumed to be familiar with Leonardo's charcoal-drawing. Amerigo Vespucci was born in 1451, and was therefore about the same age as Leonardo ; he left Florence for Spain when he was forty, and never came back to Italy, as far as is known. Though I cannot discover where and when Leonardo could have drawn the likeness of the aged Amerigo Vespucci, the Leonardo-like portrait in the Uffizi would seem to corroborate Vasari's statement. A portrait of Amerigo Vespucci by the hand of Domenico Ghirlandajo, now destroyed, was in Leonardo's time to be seen in the Vespucci Chapel of the Ognissanti church at Florence. (But cf. H. Brockhaus in Forsch. über Florentiner Kunstwerke, Leipzig 1902.)
The only other Vespucci, whom Leonardo might have portrayed, was Piero, the father of the beautiful Simonetta and the sworn enemy of the Medici; after the conspiracy of the Pazzi he was imprisoned for two years, and in 1480 he went to Milan, offering his services to Ludovico Sforza. But I think Vasari is right, and Leonardo drew the likeness of Amerigo and not of Piero Vespucci.*

(21) Fig. 9.   (22) Plates 72-75.

(23) Vasari's mistake ; Leonardo went to Milan in 1482.

the lute, in which that prince greatly delighted. Leonardo took his own instrument, made by himself in silver, and shaped like a horse's head, a curious and novel idea to render the harmonies more loud and sonorous, so that he surpassed all the musicians who had assembled there. Besides this he was the best reciter of improvised rhymes of his time. The duke, captivated by Leonardo's conversation and genius, conceived an extraordinary affection for him. He begged him to paint an altar-picture of the Nativity, which was sent by the duke to the emperor.(24) Leonardo then did a Last Supper for the Dominicans at Santa Maria delle Grazie in Milan, endowing the heads of the Apostles with such majesty and beauty that he left that of Christ unfinished, feeling that he could not give it that celestial divinity which it demanded.(25) This work left in such a condition has always been held in the greatest veneration by the Milanese and also by foreigners, as Leonardo has seized the moment when the Apostles are anxious to discover who would betray their Master. All their faces are expressive of love, fear, wrath or grief at not being able to grasp the meaning of Christ, in contrast to the obstinacy, hatred and treason of Judas, while the whole work, down to the smallest details, displays incredible diligence, even the texture of the tablecloth being clearly visible so that actual cambric would not look more real.

It is said that the prior incessantly importuned Leonardo to finish the work, thinking it strange that the artist should pass half a day at a time lost in thought. He would have desired him never to lay down the brush, as if he were digging a garden. Seeing that his importunity produced no effect, he had recourse to the duke, who felt compelled to send for Leonardo to inquire about the work, showing tactfully that he was driven to act by the importunity of the prior. Leonardo, aware of the acuteness and discretion of the duke, talked with him fully about the picture, a thing which he had never done with the prior. He spoke freely of his art, and explained how men of genius really are doing most when they work least, as they are thinking out ideas and perfecting the conceptions, which they subsequently carry out with their hands. He added that there were still two heads to be done, that of Christ, which he would not look for on the earth, and felt unable to conceive the beauty of the celestial grace that must have been incarnate in the divinity. The other head was that of Judas, which also caused him thought, as he did not think he could express the face of a man who could resolve to betray his Master, the Creator of the world, after having received so many benefits.(26) But he was willing in this case to seek no farther, and for lack of a better he would do the head

(24) Now lost. Cf. the note to plate 81.

(25) Plates 90-96 ; and 17-21.   (26) Fig. 11.

of the importunate and tactless prior. The duke was wonderfully amused, and laughingly declared that he was quite right. Then the poor prior, covered with confusion, went back to his garden and left Leonardo in peace, while the artist indeed finished his Judas, making him a veritable likeness of treason and cruelty. The head of Christ was left unfinished, as I have said. The nobility of this painting, in its composition and the care with which it was finished, induced the King of France to wish to take it home with him. Accordingly he employed architects to frame it in wood and iron, so that it might be transported in safety, without any regard for the cost, so great was his desire. But the King was thwarted by its being done on the wall, and it remained with the Milanese.

While engaged upon the Last Supper, Leonardo painted the portrait of Duke Ludovico, with Maximilian, his eldest son, at the top of this same refectory, where there is a Passion in the old style. At the other end he did the Duchess Beatrice with Francesco, her other son, both of whom afterwards became dukes of Milan, the portraits being marvellous.(27)

a profound philosopher, who then professed at Padua and wrote upon the subject.(30) I have heard it said that he was one of the first who began to illustrate the science of medicine, by the learning of Galen, and to throw true light upon anatomy, up to that time involved in the thick darkness of ignorance. In this he was marvellously served by the genius, work and hands of Leonardo, who made a book about it with red crayon drawings outlined with the pen, in which he foreshortened and portrayed with the utmost diligence. He did the skeleton, adding all the nerves and muscles, the first attached to the bone, the others keeping it firm and the third moving, and in the various parts he wrote notes in curious characters, using his left hand, and writing from right to left, so that it cannot be read without practice, and only at a mirror.(31) A great part of the sheets of this anatomy is in the hands of Messer Francesco da Melzi, a nobleman of Milan, who was a lovely child in Leonardo's time, who was very fond of him, and being now a handsome and courteous old man, he treasures up these drawings with a portrait of Leonardo.(32) Whoever succeeds in reading

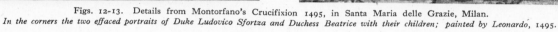

Figs. 12-13. Details from Montorfano's Crucifixion 1495, in Santa Maria delle Grazie, Milan.
In the corners the two effaced portraits of Duke Ludovico Sforza and Duchess Beatrice with their children; painted by Leonardo, 1495.

While thus employed, Leonardo suggested that the duke should set up a bronze horse of colossal size with the duke upon it in memory of himself. But he began it on such a scale that it could never be done.(28) Such is the malice of man when stirred by envy that there are some who believe that Leonardo, as with so many of his things, began this with no intention of completing it, because its size was so great that extraordinary difficulties might be foreseen in having it cast all in one piece. And it is probable that many have formed this opinion from the result, since so many of his things have been left unfinished. However, we can readily believe that his great and extraordinary talents suffered a check from being too venturesome, and that the real cause was his endeavour to go on from excellence to excellence and from perfection to perfection. "Thus the wish retarded the work", as our Petrarca says. In truth, those who have seen Leonardo's large clay model aver that they never beheld anything finer or more superb. It was preserved until the French came to Milan with King Louis of France, and broke it all to pieces. Thus a small wax model, considered perfect, was lost, as well as a book of the anatomy of horses,(29) done by him. He afterwards devoted even greater care to the study of the anatomy of men, aiding and being aided by Messer Marcantonio della Torre,

these notes of Leonardo will be amazed to find how well that divine spirit has reasoned of the arts, the muscles, the nerves and veins, with the greatest diligence in all things. N.N.,(33) a painter of Milan, also possesses some writings of Leonardo, written in the same way, which treat of painting and of the methods of design and colour. Not long ago he came to Florence to see me, wishing to

(27) *The "Crucifixion", painted by Montorfano, 1495. Leonardo added the portraits of Ludovico Sforza and his family in oil-paint over the two lower corners of the fresco. These portraits are now effaced and only their outlines are recognizable (figs. 12 and 13).*

(28) *See Plates 138-141 ; 143. The statue was not intended for Ludovico, but for his father, Francesco Sforza. The bronze horse is mentioned in Leonardo's famous letter to the Duke Ludovico, written probably in 1482 : "Again, the bronze horse may be taken in hand, which is to the immortal glory and eternal honour of the prince your father, of happy memory, and of the illustrious house of Sforza." But the first sketches for this statue can be dated after 1485, and so it would seem that Leonardo did not begin this work immediately after his arrival in Milan.*

(29) *Lost, but compare some of the measured drawings of horses, for example, Windsor Nos. 12318-19.*

(30) *Marcantonio della Torre was professor of anatomy at the University of Padua and Pavia (1511) ; he died, when only thirty years old, in 1512. Leonardo's anatomical studies are in Windsor Castle (cf. Clark, pp. L-LIII. Richter II, 83). The earliest inventory of the Leonardo drawings in the Royal Collection confirms the collaboration therein of Marcantonio della Torre (Richter II, 399). The first scientific appreciation of Leonardo's anatomical researches came from William Hunter, "Two introductory Lectures to his last course of anatomical lectures", London 1784. (See Prof. William Wright, in Burlington Magazine, May, 1919.)*

(31) *Three other contemporaries of Leonardo confirm his lefthandedness : Luca Pacioli, Sabba da Castiglione and Angelo de Beatis. Leonardo wrote from right to left, forming the letters in the reversed way, as normal writing appears in a mirror. Using his left hand, he shaded the drawings from left to right.*

(32) *Franceso Melzi, a nobleman of Milan, born 1493, died in Milan about 1570. He was a pupil and friend of Leonardo. He stayed with him in Rome (1513-15), and afterwards accompanied him to France. He was the executor of Leonardo's Will, and the Master bequeathed to him his library, his manuscripts, his instruments, some money, and even his clothes. In the Ambrosiana at Milan there are several drawings by Melzi ; the "Vertumnus and Pomona", in the Berlin Museum, the "Columbine", in the Leningrad Hermitage, and some other paintings are attributed to him.*

(33) *Vasari does not give the owner's name. As the manuscript is not mentioned at all in the first edition of his "Vite", he can only have seen it between 1551 and 1567.*

have the work printed. He afterwards went to Rome to put it in hand, but I do not know with what result.(34)

To return to Leonardo's works. When Leonardo was at Milan the King of France came there and desired him to do something curious; accordingly he made a lion whose chest opened after he had walked a few steps, discovering himself to be full of lilies.(35) At Milan Leonardo took Salai(36) of that city as his pupil. This was a graceful and beautiful youth with fine curly hair, in which Leonardo greatly delighted. He taught him many things in art, and some works which are attributed in Milan to Salai were retouched by Leonardo.(37)

Fig. 14. Lorenzo di Credi: Self-Portrait, c. 1492. Washington, National Gallery of Art (Widener Collection).

Credi, Leonardo's co-pupil in Verrocchio's studio and much influenced by him. (See fig. 24.)

Fig. 15. Leonardo: Portrait of Salai, red chalk drawing on red paper, c. 1496. Windsor Castle, Royal Library (No. 12554).

The drawing shows Salai (Giacomo Andrea, or Gian Giacomo Caprotti) at the age of about sixteen; a classical but disagreeable profile.

He returned to Florence,(38) where he found that the Servite friars had allotted to Filippino the picture of the high altar of the Annunziata. At this Leonardo declared that he should like to have done a similar thing. Filippino heard this, and being very courteous, he withdrew. The friars, wishing Leonardo to paint it, brought him to their house, paying all his expenses and those of his household. He kept them like this for a long time, but never began anything.(39) At length he drew a cartoon of the Virgin and St Anne with a Christ, which not only filled every artist with wonder, but, when it was finished and set up in the room, men and women, young and old, flocked to see it for two days, as if it had been a festival, and they marvelled exceedingly. The face of the Virgin displays all the simplicity and beauty which can shed grace on

the Mother of God, showing the modesty and humility of a Virgin contentedly happy, in seeing the beauty of her Son, whom she tenderly holds in her lap. As she regards it the little St John at her feet is caressing a lamb, while St Anne smiles in her great joy at seeing her earthly progeny become divine, a conception worthy of the great intellect and genius of Leonardo. This cartoon, as will be said below, afterwards went to France.(40) He drew Ginevra,(41) the daughter of Amerigo Benci, a beautiful portrait, and then abandoned the work of the friars, who recalled Filippino, though he was prevented from finishing it by death.(42)

For Francesco del Giocondo Leonardo undertook the portrait of Mona Lisa, his wife, and left it incomplete after working at it for four years.(43) This work is now in the possession of Francis, King of France, at Fontainebleau. This head is an extraordinary example of how art can imitate Nature, because here we have all the details painted with great subtlety. The eyes possess that moist lustre which is constantly seen in life, and about them are those livid reds and hair which cannot be rendered without the utmost delicacy. The lids could not be more natural, for the way in which the hairs issue from the skin, here thick and there scanty, and following the pores of the skin. The nose possesses the fine delicate reddish apertures seen in life. The opening of the mouth, with its red ends, and the scarlet cheeks seem not colour but living flesh. To look closely at her throat you might imagine that the pulse was beating. Indeed, we may say that this was painted in a manner to cause the boldest artists to despair. Mona Lisa was very beautiful, and while Leonardo was drawing her portrait he engaged people to play and sing, and jesters to keep her merry, and remove that melancholy which painting usually gives to portraits. This figure of Leonardo's has such a pleasant smile that it seemed rather divine

(40) *See Suida, Leonardo und sein Kreis, pp. 130-131.—This first cartoon of the Virgin and St Anne was finished in 1501, but it is lost, and we know it only from a description given by Fra Pietro da Novellara. Cf. our notes on plates 22, 87, 88.*

(41) *Plate 23.*

(42) *Now in the Florence Academy, No. 98. Finished 1504 by Perugino.*

(43) *1502-1506.—Plate 26.*

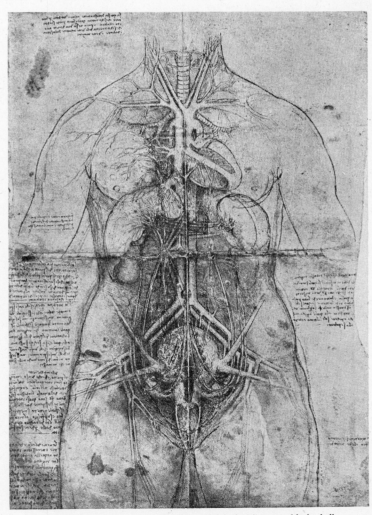

Fig. 16. Leonardo: Anatomical study, pen and ink drawing over black chalk, c. 1513. Windsor Castle, Royal Library (No. 12281).

Dissection of the principal organs, and the arterial system of a female figure.

(34) *The first printed edition was published in 1651 by Raphael du Fresne in Paris. The first English translation was issued (anonymously) in 1721, London. But the Trattato della Pittura is a mere compilation by some disciple. For Leonardo's Manuscripts see Bibliography, Nos. 3-6.*

(35) *An automaton, such as had been constructed ever since ancient times. Vasari's story is confirmed by Lomazzo (Trattato dell'arte, Milan, 1585, p. 106; and Idea del tempio, Milan, 1590, p. 17). Lomazzo states that he heard from Francesco Melzi that this lion was made for Francis the First. Similar sketches may be found on a sheet (fol. 179 recto) of the Codice Atlantico (published by Müller-Walde, Prussian Jahrbuch, 1898, p. 233). Lomazzo was also told that Leonardo constructed artificial birds which flew through the air—similar automatons were made by the Emperor Charles the Fifth on his retirement to the cloister of San Geronimo de Yuste.*

(36) *Giacomo Salai came to live with Leonardo as a boy of ten, on the 22nd July, 1490. He was obviously a child of bad character—Leonardo called him "thief, liar, glutton". But the Master kept him for twenty-five years, gave him expensive presents, including a cloak of silver brocade, trimmed with green velvet, and a pair of rose-coloured tights; nor did he forget him in his Will. Emil Möller (Salai und Leonardo, in the Vienna Jahrbuch, NF II, 1928, p. 139 et seq.) attributed a number of beautiful paintings to Salai.*

(37) *A letter from the White Friar, Pietro da Novellara, to Isabella d'Este, 1501, states that Leonardo corrected and retouched the paintings of his pupils (cf. fig. 20 and plates 28, 31, 70).*

(38) *24th April 1500.*

(39) *See W. R. Valentiner, Über zwei Kompositionen Leonardos, in the Prussian Jahrbuch, vol. 56, 1935, p. 213 et seq.*

than human, and was considered marvellous, an exact copy of Nature.

The fame of this divine artist grew to such a pitch by the excellence of his works that all who delighted in the arts and the whole city wished him to leave some memorial, and they endeavoured to think of some noteworthy decorative work through which the State might be adorned and honoured by the genius, grace and judgment characteristic of his work. The great hall of the council was being rebuilt under the direction of Giuliano da San Gallo, Simone Pollajuolo called Cronaca, Michelangelo Buonarroti and Baccio d'Agnolo, by the judgment and advice of the gonfaloniere,(44) and leading citizens, as will be related at greater length in another place, and being finished with great speed, it was ordained by public decree that Leonardo should be employed to paint some fine work. Thus the hall was allotted to him by Piero Soderini, then gonfaloniere of justice. Leonardo began by drawing a cartoon at the hall of the Pope,(45) a place in Santa Maria Novella, containing the story of Niccolo Piccinino, captain of Duke Filippo of Milan.(46) Here he designed a group of horsemen fighting for a standard, a masterly work on account of his treatment of the fight, displaying the wrath, anger and vindictiveness of men

Fig. 18. "The Fight for the Standard". Part of Leonardo's "The Battle of Anghiari," 1505. Engraving by Gerard Edelinck, c. 1680, after a Flemish copy in the Louvre.

and horses; two of the latter, with their front legs involved, are waging war with their teeth no less fiercely than their riders are fighting for the standard. One soldier, putting his horse to the gallop, has turned round and, grasping the staff of the standard, is endeavouring by main force to wrench it from the hands of four others, while two are defending it, trying to cut the staff with their swords; an old soldier in a red cap has a hand on the staff, as he cries out, and holds a scimetar in the other and threatens to cut off both hands of the two, who are grinding their teeth and making every effort to defend their banner. On the ground, between the legs of the horses, are two foreshortened figures who are fighting together, while a soldier lying prone has another over him who is raising his arm as high as he can to run his dagger with his utmost strength into his adversary's throat; the latter, whose legs and arms are helpless, does what he can to escape death. The manifold designs Leonardo made for the costumes of his soldiers defy description, not to speak of the scimetars and other ornaments, and his incredible

mastery of form and line in dealing with horses, which he made better than any other master, with their powerful muscles and graceful beauty. It is said that for designing the cartoon he made an ingenious scaffolding which rose higher when pressed together and broadened out when lowered. Thinking that he could paint on the wall in oils, he made a composition so thick for laying on the wall that when he continued his painting it began to run and spoil what had been begun, so that in a short time he was forced to abandon it.(47)

Leonardo had a high spirit and was most generous in every action. It is said that when he went to the bank for the monthly provision that he used to receive from Piero Soderini, the cashier wanted to give him some rolls of farthings, but he would not take them, saying that he was not a painter for farthings. Learning that Piero Soderini accused him of deceiving him and that murmurs rose against him, Leonardo with the help of his friends collected the money and took it back, but Piero would not accept it. He went to Rome(48) with Duke Giuliano de' Medici on the election of Leo X, who studied philosophy and especially alchemy. On the way he made a paste with wax and constructed hollow animals which flew in the air when blown up, but fell when the wind ceased. On a curious lizard found by the vine-dresser of Belvedere he fastened scales taken from other lizards, dipped in quicksilver, which trembled as it moved, and after giving it eyes, a horn and a beard, he tamed it and kept it in a box. All the friends to whom he showed it ran away terrified. He would often dry and purge the guts of a wether and make them so small that they might be held in the palm of the hand. In another room he kept a pair of smith's bellows, and with these he would blow out one of the guts until it filled the room, which was a large one, forcing anyone there to take refuge in a corner. The fact that it had occupied such a little space at first only added to the wonder. He perpetrated many such follies, studied mirrors and made curious experiments to find oil for painting and varnish to preserve the work done. At this time he did a small picture for Messer Baldassare Turini of Pescia, the datary of Leo, of the Virgin and Child, with infinite diligence and art.(49) But to-day it is much spoiled either by neglect or because of his numerous fanciful mixtures and the colouring. In another picture he represented a little child, marvellously beautiful and graceful, both works being now at Pescia in the possession of Messer Giulio Turini.(50) It is said that, on being commissioned by the Pope to do a work, he straightway began to distil oil and herbs to make the varnish, which induced Pope Leo to say: "This man will never do anything, for he begins to think of the end before the beginning!"

There was no love lost between him and Michelangelo Buonarroti, so that the latter left Florence owing to their rivalry, Duke Giuliano excusing him by saying that he was summoned by the Pope to do the façade of San Lorenzo.(51) When Leonardo heard this, he left for France, where the king had heard of his works and wanted him to do the cartoon of St Anne in colours.(52) But Leonardo, as was his wont, gave him nothing but words for a long time. At length, having become old, he lay sick for many months, and seeing himself near death, he desired to occupy himself with the truths of the Catholic Faith and the holy Christian religion. Then, having confessed and shown his penitence with much lamentation, he devoutly took the Sacrament out of his bed, supported by his friends and servants, as he could not stand. The king arriving, for he would often pay him friendly visits, he sat up in bed from respect, and related the circumstances of his sickness, showing how greatly he had offended God and man in not having worked in his art as he ought. He was then seized with a paroxysm, the harbinger of

(44) Gonfaloniere di Giustizia, the "standard-bearer of justice", the highest Florentine magistrate. In the Life of Cronaca Vasari says: "At the same time it was proposed to make the great hall of the Signoria at Florence for the council of Fra Girolamo Savonarola, the famous preacher [July, 1495]. Upon this a consultation was held with Leonardo da Vinci, Michelangelo Buonarroti, then a youth, Giuliano da San Gallo, Baccio d'Agnolo and Simone Pollajuolo, called Cronaca. . . After many discussions it was agreed that the hall should be made as it always stood until its restoration in our own day." If this statement of Vasari's is correct, Leonardo was for some time in Florence before he started the work on the Last Supper in Milan.

(45) Thus called because this part of the Convent was the abode of different Popes during the 15th and 16th centuries.

(46) The Battle of Anghiari, 29th June 1440; a victory of the Florentines over the Pisans.

(47) Plates 6, 7; 129-136; fig. 18. The original cartoon, on which Leonardo worked from October 1503 till February 1505, is lost, as also is the mural which had to give way to one of Vasari's paintings when the room was redecorated in 1565.

(48) 24th September 1513; in August 1516 he was still there.

(49) Lost.

(50) Probably the Infant Jesus. The picture is lost; Rio thought that it was burnt in Whitehall.

(51) Michelangelo left Florence in December 1516, when Duke Giuliano was no longer alive, and Leonardo was on his way to France.

(52) Plates 87-89A.

death, so that the king rose and took his head to assist him and show him favour as well as to alleviate the pain. Leonardo's divine spirit, then recognising that he could not enjoy a greater honour, expired in the king's arms, at the age of seventy-five.(53)

The loss of Leonardo caused exceptional grief to those who had known him, because there never was a man who did so much honour to painting. By the splendour of his magnificent mien he comforted every sad soul, and his eloquence could turn men to either side of a question. His personal strength was prodigious, and with his right hand he could bend the clapper of a knocker or a horseshoe as if they had been of lead. His liberality warmed the hearts of all his friends, both rich and poor, if they possessed talent and ability. His presence adorned and honoured the most wretched and bare apartment. Thus Florence received a great gift in the birth of Leonardo, and its loss in his death was immeasurable.

To the art of painting in oil he added a certain mode of deepening the shadows, whereby the moderns have imparted great vigour and relief to their figures. He proved his powers in statuary in three figures in bronze over the door of San Giovanni on the north side. They were executed by Giovan Francesco Rustici, but

Fig. 19. Gian Francesco Rustici (with the help of Leonardo): The Baptist between a Pharisee and a Levite, 1506-11. Bronze group over the north door of the Florentine Baptistery.

under Leonardo's direction, and are the finest casts for design and general perfection that have as yet been seen.(54) To Leonardo we owe a greater perfection in the anatomy of horses and men.

---

(53) *Leonardo died on May 2nd, 1519, when sixty-seven years old. A letter from Francesco Melzi from Amboise, dated June 1st, 1519, to Leonardo's brothers, does not mention the King, who, on the day of Leonardo's death, was, in fact, not in Amboise, but with the Court at St Germain-en-Laye. (Document XVII.)*

(54) *Fig. 19.—Rustici received the commission for this work towards the end of 1506 and worked on it till September 1509, when he began the casting in bronze. Leonardo stayed in Florence from September 1507 to June 1508, living in Piero di Braccio Martelli's house, in which was also Rustici's studio. (Cf. note on plate 150.) In the Life of Baccio Bandinelli Vasari gives some further information: "Baccio's father, perceiving his son's bent... put the boy in charge of Giovan Francesco Rustici, one of the best sculptors of the city, where Leonardo continually practised... Encouraged by Leonardo's advice, Baccio began to copy an ancient marble head of a woman which he had modelled from one in the Medici palace." Here we see Leonardo giving advice to a young apprentice in Rustici's studio. In the Life of Rustici we read: "Rustici learned much from Leonardo, especially in making horses, of which he was very fond, producing them in clay, in wax, in full and in bas-relief, and every imaginable way... As he lived awhile in the via de' Martelli, he was very friendly with the family." This happened when Leonardo was staying in the Martelli family's house, 1507-1508. In the same chapter Vasari supplies more detailed information about Leonardo's help with Rustici's bronze group over the door of the Florence baptistery (fig. 19): "While engaged upon this work Rustici would allow no one near save Leonardo da Vinci, who never left him while he was moulding and casting until the work was finished. Many therefore believe, though nothing definite is known, that Leonardo worked at them himself, or at least helped Rustici with his advice and judgment".*

Thus, by his many surpassing gifts, even though he talked much more about his works than he actually achieved, his name and fame will never be extinguished. Therefore Messer Giovan Battista Strozzi wrote thus in his praise :

> *Vince costui pur solo*
> *Tutti altri, e vince Fidia e vince Apelle,*
> *E tutto il lor vittorioso stuolo.*(55)

Giovan Antonio Boltraffio(56) of Milan was a pupil of Leonardo, and a very skilful and intelligent man, who in 1500 painted a panel in oils in the church of the Misericordia, outside Bologna, with the Virgin and Child, St John the Baptist, and a nude St Sebastian, including a portrait of the donor kneeling. (57) To this fine work he signed his name, adding that he was a pupil of Leonardo. He did other works at Milan and elsewhere, but the one I have just referred to is the best. Marco Uggioni,(58) another pupil, painted the Death of the Virgin and the Marriage of Cana in Galilee in Santa Maria della Pace.(59)

---

(55) *"He alone vanquished all others, he surpassed Phidias, surpassed Appelles, and all their proud followers."* Here again is a play on the words Vinci *and* vincere.

(56) *Born 1467, died 1516. (Cf. Fig. 20 and Plate 28.)*

(57) *Now in the Louvre, No. 1169 ; painted in 1500, for the Casio family. According to an old tradition (Baldinucci) Leonardo himself helped with the painting.*

(58) *Marco d'Oggione (or d'Oggiono), born about 1470 at Oggiono near Milan ; worked in Leonardo's studio in or before 1490 ; died in Milan about 1530. The copy he made of Leonardo's "Last Supper", now at The Royal Academy, London, is well known.*

(59) *The two pictures are now in the Brera, Milan ; Nos. 79 and 81.*

Fig. 20. Boltraffio (with the help of Leonardo ?): Madonna with the flower-pot, c. 1498. Budapest, Museum of Fine Arts,

ADDITIONAL REFERENCES CONCERNING LEONARDO DA VINCI · TAKEN FROM DIFFERENT "VITE" BY VASARI · 1568

In the "Life of Giorgione":

Having seen and greatly admired some things of Leonardo, richly toned and exceedingly dark, as has been said, Giorgione made them his model, and imitated them carefully in painting in oil. (60).

(60) "Exceedingly dark" connects Giorgione's first style with Leonardo's "chiaroscuro", mentioned in his Life by Vasari (p. 13). Leonardo passed through Venice in 1500 and 1503 (and perhaps in 1506). "But in 1507," says Vasari in the Life of Titian, "arose Giorgione, who began to give his works more tone and relief, with better style." How far the young Giorgione made him his model can be seen from his "Christ carrying the Cross" (cf. note on plate 91), but still more from his "Judith" in the Hermitage, which seems to me more Leonardesque than all the copies of the standing "Leda" attributed to the School of Leonardo. Leonardo's knot pattern is used as an ornament on the dress of the Brocardo portrait by Giorgione in the Budapest Museum.

In the "Life of Andrea del Verrocchio":

There are some of Andrea's drawings in our possession. . . among them being some female heads so beautiful and with such charming hair that Leonardo was always imitating them.

We have besides two [drawings of] horses, squared and with measured proportions, by which method they can be increased to a larger scale without error. (61)

(61) Some of Verrocchio's drawings are sometimes attributed to Leonardo; e.g. a most charming head in the British Museum (fig. 68); the famous silverpoint drawing in Dresden, connected with the Pistoja altar-piece (reproduced e.g. Morelli, Munich and Dresden, p. 266); a Madonna head in Paris (repr. Suida, pl. 4); and others.

In the "Life of Piero di Cosimo":

He practised painting in oil after seeing some things by Leonardo toned and finished with the extreme diligence characteristic of that Master when he wished to display his art. This method pleased Piero, and he strove to imitate it, though he was a long way behind Leonardo. (62)

(62) Piero di Cosimo borrowed from Leonardo's Madonna drawings. Suida contends that his painting "Perseus and Andromeda" in the

Fig. 21. Piero di Cosimo: Perseus and Andromeda, Detail, c. 1508. Florence, Uffizi.
According to an old tradition painted by Piero after a design by Leonardo. There is a similar drawing of a dragon at Windsor (No. 12369); the curious musical instruments recall the one which Leonardo took with him to Milan, as Vasari states, "made by himself in silver, and shaped like a horse's head."

Florence Uffizi is taken completely from a drawing by Leonardo, or even executed with his help. He was not the first to express this opinion. In the inventory of the Uffizi Gallery, made in 1580, the picture is mentioned as drawn by Leonardo and coloured by Piero di Cosimo. Morelli (Galleries in Rome, Engl. ed., 1892, p. 120) said "Several of the heads have not only Leonardo's sfumato, but recall the Gioconda in expression." And Maud Cruttwell (A Guide to the Paintings in the Florentine Galleries, 1907, p. 98): "The female crouched in the foreground with a strange-shaped musical instrument is worthy of Leonardo, who it is not impossible may have designed it." But Morelli rightly emphasized that there is no question but that the composition is by Piero di Cosimo, and not by Leonardo. The drawing of a reclining Venus in the same collection, published as a drawing by Verrocchio, and recently as by Leonardo, is, I think, by Piero (Reproduced, e.g. Cruttwell, Verrocchio, pl. VII, pp. 5 & 6). See fig. 21.

In the "Life of Fra Bartolommeo":

After leaving Cosimo Rosselli, he began earnestly to study the paintings of Leonardo da Vinci, and in a short time made such progress in colouring that he became known as one of the best of the young artists both for colour and design. (63)

(63) Leonardo's influence is visible only in Bartolommeo's early work, before his stay in Venice, 1508. "His assiduous study of body and drapery shows the spirit of Leonardo," as K. Escher expressed it.

In the Chapter on "Lombard Artists":

In the Mint at Milan there is a copy of a portrait of a smiling woman by Leonardo done by Frà Girolamo [Monsignori] and of a young St John the Baptist, very well imitated. (64)

(64) This passage from Vasari shows that even in the middle of the 16th century it was not easy to distinguish Leonardo's work from imitations.

In the "Life of Raphael":

In his childhood Raphael imitated the style of Pietro Perugino, his master, improving it greatly in design, colouring and invention. But in riper years he perceived that this was too far from the truth. For he saw the works of Leonardo da Vinci, who had no equal in the expression which he gave to his heads of women and children, while in the grace and movement of his figures he surpassed all other artists; this filled Raphael with wonder and amazement. As Leonardo's style pleased him more than any he had ever seen, he set to work to study it, and gradually and painfully abandoning the manner of Pietro, he sought as far as possible to imitate Leonardo; and, though some consider him superior in sweetness, and in a certain natural facility, yet he never excelled that wonderful groundwork of ideas and that grandeur of art, in which few have equalled Leonardo. Raphael, however, approached him more closely than any other painter, especially in grace of colouring. (65)

(65) How much Raphael borrowed from Leonardo cannot be told in a single note. He was indebted to Leonardo's Anghiari cartoon, his standing Leda with the Swan, and his Mona Lisa. From his drawing after the Mona Lisa, Raphael painted his portrait of Maddalena Doni, while his portrait of the Madonna Gravida in the Palazzo Pitti at Florence is obviously an adaptation of "La Monaca di Leonardo", in the Uffizi, a painting now usually ascribed to Ridolfo Ghirlandaio, but, as I believe, certainly a copy of a lost portrait by Leonardo. Raphael's "Family with the Lamb" is copied freely from Leonardo's first St Anne cartoon; his Madonna with the Flower, his Esterházy Madonna, his Madonna Alba, in fact most of his Madonna paintings are either directly derived from drawings by Leonardo, or are variations of them. It may sound paradoxical, but it seems that Leonardo had only two true disciples: Raphael and Dürer.

Fig. 22. "La Monaca di Leonardo", by an unknown, Florentine painter (copy after Leonardo? c. 1503). Florence Uffizi.

Fig. 23. Raphael: Donna Gravida, c. 1505. Florence, Palazzo Pitti. (*Background repainted. Not only same composition, but probably also same model as in Fig. 22*).

In the "*Life of Lorenzo di Credi*":

His ambition rising, Lorenzo went to Andrea del Verrocchio, whose whim was then painting. Under this master he had as friends and companions, although rivals, Pietro Perugino and Leonardo da Vinci, both diligently studying painting. Leonardo's style greatly delighted Lorenzo, who succeeded better than any others in imitating his polish and finish. (66)

Lorenzo's first work was a circular painting (tondo) of a Madonna sent to the King of Spain, the design being taken from one of Andrea del Verrocchio's. He then did a far better picture, copied from one by Leonardo da Vinci, and also sent to Spain. It could not be distinguished from the original.

(66) *Some works of Lorenzo di Credi were sometimes ascribed to Leonardo, and vice versa. Thus, for instance, the Liechtenstein portrait (plate 23), the Munich Madonna (plate 68), the Benois Madonna (plate 65), the Uffizi Annunciation (plate 66) were once attributed to Credi. On the other hand, the predella of the Pistoja altar-piece: the Louvre Annunciation (fig. 24), and "San Donato of Arezzo and the Tax Collector"*

in the Collection of Theodore T. Ellis. Worcester, Mass., U.S.A., were thought to be by Leonardo. The Pistoja altar-piece was produced in Verrocchio's workshop, 1475-1485; it was begun by the Master himself but finished by Credi. Leonardo probably had a share in it. (Cf. notes on plates 68, 99 and 115.) About eight years older than Credi, Leonardo was not only his co-pupil in Verrochio's workshop but his teacher as well.

In the "*Life of Piero della Francesca*":

And although Time, which is called the father of Truth, sooner or later brings the truth to light, yet they are for some time defrauded of the honour due to their labours. This was the case with Piero della Francesca of Borgo a San Sepolcro, who, being considered a consummate arithmetician, geometrician and perspectivist, was nevertheless prevented—first by the blindness, which came upon him in his old age, and finally by the termination of his life—from displaying the results of his labours and of the numerous books written by him, which are still preserved

Fig. 24. Lorenzo di Credi (with the help of Leonardo?): Annunciation. Part of the predella of the Pistoja Altar-piece, c. 1481. Paris, Louvre.
The Pistoja Altar-piece was begun in 1475, in Verrocchio's workshop; in 1478, when Leonardo was in Pistoja, it was nearly finished; but the last touches were not done until 1485, and certainly by Lorenzo di Credi.

in his native Borgo. The man who should have done his utmost to increase Piero's glory and reputation, who had learned from him everything which he knew, impiously and malignantly sought to annul his teacher's fame, and usurp the honour due to him, publishing under his own name of Frà Luca dal Borgo all the results of the labours of that good old man, who, besides his knowledge mentioned above, was also an excellent painter...

Piero was, as I have said, a diligent student of his art who assiduously practised perspective, and had a thorough acquaintance with Euclid, so that he understood better than anyone else all the curves in regular bodies and we owe to him the fullest light that had been thrown on the subject. It happened thus: Luca dal Borgo, a Franciscan friar, who wrote of regular bodies in geometry, was his pupil; and when Piero came to his old age and died, after having written many books, the same master Luca took upon himself to have them printed as his own, since they came into his hands on his master's death...

The majority of Piero's books are in the library of Federigo II, Duke of Urbino, and their excellences have earned him the well-deserved reputation of being the best geometrician of his day. (67)

(67) *Piero della Francesca (c. 1416-1492) wrote two treatises on perspective and the art of drawing. The one mentioned by Vasari as being in the library of the Duke of Urbino is now in the Biblioteca Vaticana at Rome (Codex Urbinas 652, "Petri Pictoris Burgensis de quinque corporibus regularibus"); the best manuscript of the other treatise is in the Biblioteca Palatina at Parma (Cod. Cart. No. 1576, "De prospectiva pingendi"). Luca Pacioli—whom Vasari calls Luca dal Borgo—did not plagiarize the work of Piero, as he repeatedly acknowledges the priority of his teacher's "prospectiva pingendi" in his "Summa Arithmetica", Venice 1494. The other man from whom Luca Pacioli learned at one period was Leon Battista Alberti, in whose house at Rome he stayed in 1471. Alberti was the author of "Three books on painting" (1435), in which, among other things, he teaches the difference between studio light and plein-air, the perspective of colours, and reflection in sunlight. Luca Pacioli was Leonardo's friend. From 1496 onwards he was in Milan teaching mathematics. When, in 1499, Leonardo fled from Milan to Mantua and Venice, he was accompanied by Luca Pacioli. In Venice, in 1509, Luca Pacioli published his "De Divina Proportione", with sixty illustrations from designs by Leonardo. It was Luca Pacioli who transmitted the theories of Piero della Francesca and Leon Battista Alberti to Leonardo. (See fig. 25.)*

TWO PASSAGES FROM THE "LIFE OF LEONARDO" BY THE ANONIMO GADDIANO (OR MAGLIABECCHIANO), c. 1540.

(1. Leonardo and Michelangelo)

As Leonardo, accompanied by G. da Gavina, was passing the Spini bank, hard by the church of Santa Trinita, several notables were there assembled, who were discussing a passage in Dante, and seeing Leonardo, they bade him come and explain it to them. At the same moment Michelangelo passed, and on one of the crowd calling to him, Leonardo said, 'Michelangelo will be able to tell you what it means.' To which the latter, thinking this had been said to entrap him, replied, 'Nay, do thou explain it thyself, horse-modeller that thou art—who, unable to cast a statue in bronze, wast forced with shame to give up the attempt.' So saying, he turned his back upon them and departed. (68)

(68) *This incident happened probably in 1501, when Michelangelo received his commission for the "David", as Vasari hints, in competition with Leonardo. Vasari in his "Life of Michelangelo" says: "Some of Michelangelo's friends wrote from Florence urging him to return, as they did not want that block of marble in the* opera *to be spoiled which Piero Soderini, then gonfaloniere for life in the city, had frequently proposed to give to Leonardo da Vinci. . . ." (The "opera" was the office of Works for the Cathedral.)*

(2. The Appearance of Leonardo)

He had a fine figure and was well-proportioned, graceful and of handsome appearance. He used to wear a short pink cloak (*pitocco*), reaching to his knees, when long garments were the fashion of the day. He wore his beard long, curled and beautifully kept, falling down to the middle of his chest. (69)

(69) *Lomazzo (in "Tempio," p. 58) also states that Leonardo had long hair and eye-brows.—See plate 1, and figs. 34-45.—Leonardo cared much for fine clothes. At one time, in 1505, he paid 18 Lire for the sending of a parcel of garments, and he paid only 4 Lire for paint and oil. Paolo Giovo says of him: "He was the arbiter of all questions relating to elegance and beauty." Leonardo was certainly the arbiter elegantiarum at the Court of Milan, and in some ways even the* maître de plaisir.

Fig. 25. Portrait of Luca Pacioli, with a noble disciple. Dated 1495, attributed to Jacopo de' Barbari. Naples, Museo Nazionale.
On the book-case on the right the inscription: LI(tteratus) R(arus) LUC(as) BVR(gensis)—(*The excellent scholar Luca of Borgo*).
(*Cf. note 67*)

LETTERS AND OTHER DOCUMENTS

I. Draft of a letter from Leonardo to Ludovico Sforza, in which he offers his services and states his abilities; c. 1482.

Most Illustrious Lord, Having now sufficiently considered the specimens of all those who proclaim themselves skilled contrivers of instruments of war, and that the invention and operation of the said instruments are nothing different from those in common use : I shall endeavour, without prejudice to any one else, to explain myself to your Excellency, showing your Lordship my secrets, and then offering them to your best pleasure and approbation to work with effect at opportune moments on all those things which, in part, shall be briefly noted below.

(1) I have a sort of extremely light and strong bridges, adapted to be most easily carried, and with them you may pursue, and at any time flee from the enemy ; and others, secure and indestructible by fire and battle, easy and convenient to lift and place. Also methods of burning and destroying those of the enemy.

(2) I know how, when a place is besieged, to take the water out of the trenches, and make endless variety of bridges, and covered ways and ladders, and other machines pertaining to such expeditions.

(3) Item. If, by reason of the height of the banks, or the strength of the place, and its position, it is impossible, when besieging a place, to avail oneself of the plan of bombardment, I have methods for destroying every rock or other fortress, even if it were founded on a rock, &c.

(4) Again, I have kinds of mortars ; most convenient and easy to carry ; and with these I can fling small stones almost resembling a storm ; and with the smoke of these cause great terror to the enemy, to his great detriment and confusion.

(5) Item. I have means by secret and tortuous mines and ways, made without noise, to reach a designated [spot], even if it were needed to pass under a trench or a river.

(6) Item. I will make covered chariots, safe and unassailable, which, entering among the enemy with their artillery, there is no body of man so great but they would break them. And behind these, infantry could follow quite unhurt and without any hindrance.

(7) Item. In case of need I will make big guns, mortars, and light ordnance of fine and useful forms, out of the common type.

(8) Where the operation of bombardment might fail, I would contrive catapults, mangonels, *trabocchi*, and other machines of marvellous efficacy and not in common use. And in short, according to the variety of cases, I can contrive various and endless means of offence and defence.

(9) And if the fight should be at sea I have many kinds of machines most efficient for offence and defence ; and vessels which will resist the attack of the largest guns and powder and fumes.

(10) In time of peace I believe I can give perfect satisfaction and to the equal of any other in architecture and the composition of buildings public and private ; and in guiding water from one place to another.

Item. I can carry out sculpture in marble, bronze, or clay, and also I can do in painting whatever may be done, as well as any other, be he who he may.

Again, the bronze horse may be taken in hand, which is to be to the immortal glory and eternal honour of the prince your father of happy memory, and of the illustrious house of Sforza.

And if any of the above-named things seem to any one to be impossible or not feasible, I am most ready to make the experiment in your park, or in whatever place may please your Excellency— to whom I commend myself with the utmost humility, &c.

II. A Letter from the Florentine Ambassador in Milan to his master, Lorenzo de' Medici, 22 July, 1489 ; concerning the Sforza Monument.

The Duke Ludovico is planning to erect a worthy monument to his father, and in accordance with his orders Leonardo has been asked to make a model in the form of a large horse in bronze ridden by the Duke Francesco in full armour. As His Highness has in mind something wonderful, the like of which has never been seen, he has directed me to write to you and ask if you will kindly send him one or two Florentine artists who specialize in this kind of work. For, although the Duke has given the commission to Leonardo, it seems to me that he is not confident that he will succeed.

III. From Leonardo's Note-books, concerning the Sforza Monument.

"On the 23rd of April, 1490. . . I started the horse afresh."

IV. From the draft of a letter by Leonardo to the Duke Ludovico Sforza, c. 1498.

. . . . It vexes me greatly that having to earn my living has forced me to interrupt the work and to attend to small matters, instead of following up the work which your Lordship entrusted to me. But I hope in a short time to have earned so much that I may carry it out quietly to the satisfaction of your Excellency, to whom I commend myself ; and if your Lordship thought that I had money, your Lordship was deceived, because I had to feed 6 men for 36 months, and have had only 50 ducats.

V. Ercole I d'Este, Duke of Ferrara, to his agent in Milan, 19 September, 1501 ; Concerning the model of the Sforza Monument.

Seeing that there exists at Milan a model of a horse, executed by a certain Messer Leonardo, a master very skilful in such matters, one which the Duke Ludovico always intended to have cast, we think that, if the use were granted us of this model, it would be a good and desirable thing to make a casting from it. Therefore, we wish you to go immediately to the most illustrious and reverend the Lord Cardinal of Rouen and acquaint him with our desire, begging his reverend lordship, if he do not need the said model himself, to be so good as to make it over to us. We would not deprive him of anything that he holds valuable, yet we are persuaded that he cares but little for this work. You may add, likewise, that this will be very agreeable to us for the reasons aforesaid ; and that we would gladly be at pains to remove it, bearing in mind that the said model at Milan is, as you have told us, falling daily into decay, there being no care taken of it. If the very reverend lord will gratify us, as we hope, in this matter, we will send persons to bring the said model hither with all care and due precaution, so that it come by no hurt. Do not fail to employ all your good offices that our petition may be granted by his very reverend lordship, to whom we proffer our offers of service and our humble duty.

The Cardinal of Rouen was at that time the French governor at Milan.— A model of the equestrian monument was exhibited in 1493, on the occasion of the marriage of the Emperor Maximilian with Bianca Maria Sforza in Milan. When the French entered the town, the Gascon bowmen used this clay model as a target and destroyed it, as Sabba da Castiglione and Vasari have recorded. But, as a year later the Duke of Ferrara asked for the model of the horse, we can only assume that Leonardo had made more than one.

VI. From the answer of Giovanni Valla, the agent of Ercole I d'Este, Milan, 24 December, 1501.

With reference to the model of the horse erected by Duke Ludovico, as far as he is concerned, his reverend lordship perfectly agrees to its removal ; yet as his Majesty the King had himself seen the statue, his lordship dare not grant the Duke's request without previously informing the King.

VII. The Duke, Ludovico Sforza, to his secretary Domino Marchesino Stange ; concerning the "Last Supper".

We have entrusted to you the carrying out of the matters mentioned on the enclosed list ; and, although our orders were delivered to you by word of mouth, it shall add to our comfort that we set them down in these few words, to inform you how extraordinary is our interest in their execution.

Milan, the 30th of June, 1497. LUDOVICO MARIA SFORTIA

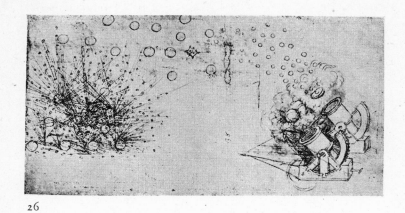

26

29

27

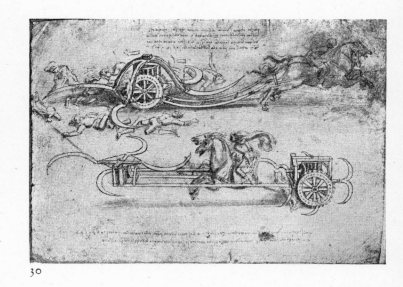

30

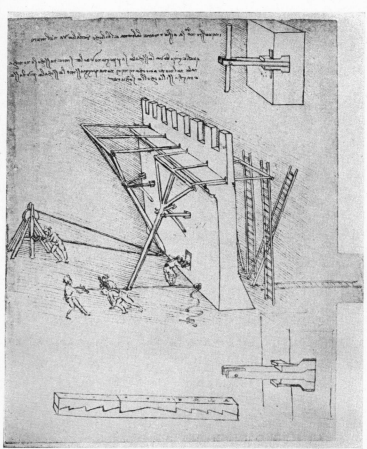

28

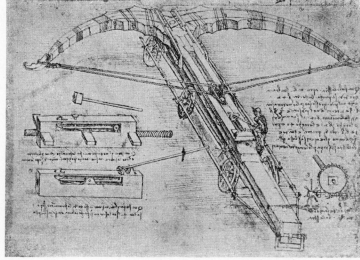

31

Figs. 26-31. Leonardo : Designs of Machines of War, 1482-85.—(26) Mortars. Codex Atlanticus, 9r.-a. Biblioteca Ambrosiana, Milan.—(27) Archers, explosive shells, etc. Paris, Ecole des Beaux-Arts.—(28) Device against storm ladders. Codex Atlanticus, 49v.-b.—(29) War machine with scythes and covered chariot or tank. British Museum.—(30) War-chariots with scythes. Turin, Royal Library.—(31) "Ballista", a huge cross-bow. Codex Atlanticus, 53v.-b.

The "memoriale" appended to this letter mentions thirteen different matters, the greater portion referring to works of art. One of the points is:

"Item. Of Leonardo of Florence it is to be solicited that he finish the work in the Refettorio delle Gratie, when he must set to work upon the other front wall thereof, which if he can do, the agreements previously signed by him respecting its completion within a given time will be cancelled."

VIII. CONCERNING THE "LAST SUPPER". FROM A TALE BY MATTEO BANDELLO ("NOVELLE", LUCCA 1554).

In Ludovico's time, some gentlemen living in Milan were met one day in the monks' refectory of the convent delle Grazie, where with hushed voices they watched Leonardo da Vinci as he was finishing his marvellous picture of the *Last Supper*. The painter was well pleased that each should tell him what they thought of his work. He would often come to the convent at early dawn; and this I have seen him do myself. Hastily mounting the scaffolding, he worked diligently until the shades of evening compelled him to cease, never thinking to take food at all, so absorbed was he in his work. At other times he would remain there three or four days without touching his picture, only coming for a few hours to remain before it, with folded arms, gazing at his figures as if to criticise them himself. At mid-day, too, when the glare of a sun at its zenith has made barren all the streets of Milan, I have seen him hasten from the citadel, where he was modelling his colossal horse, without seeking the shade, by the shortest way to the convent, where he would add a touch or two and immediately return.

Bandello was a nephew of Vincenzo, the prior of the Dominican monastery of Santa Maria delle Grazie. In 1495, when he was about fifteen, he came to Milan and was placed in the care of his uncle; two years later he became acquainted with Leonardo, who was then painting the "Last Supper" in the refectory of the Church belonging to the monks whose prior was Bandello's uncle. One of Bandello's tragical stories was the original of "Romeo and Juliet".

IX. LEONARDO IN VENICE. A LETTER OF THE AMBASSADOR OF MANTUA, CONCERNING THE PORTRAIT OF ISABELLA D'ESTE.

Most illustrious Lady,

Leonardo da Vinci, who is in Venice, has shewed to me a portrait of your Highness, which is in every way a most truthful likeness. Indeed it is so well executed that nothing could be better. This is all that I write by this post, and with the repeated assurance of my respect,

I beg to subscribe myself,

Your Highness's faithful servant,

LORENZO DA PAVIA

Venice, 13th March, 1500

A la illustrissima Madamma Elisabetta Marchesana de Mantova.

Leonardo's portrait of Isabella d'Este is mentioned by Père Dan (Trésor des merveilles de Fontainebleau, 1642) as being in the collection of Francis the First, King of France.—Cf. plate 24.

X. FROM A LETTER OF ISABELLA D'ESTE, 27 MARCH, 1501, TO FRA PIETRO DA NOVELLARA; CONCERNING A MADONNA PAINTING AND A PORTRAIT.

Ascertain whether he is inclined to paint a picture in our studio. If he consents, we will leave the invention and the time to his decision. If he is reluctant, try at least to induce him to paint for us a small picture of the Madonna, pious and sweet, as is his style. And then ask him to send us a new sketch of our portrait. For his Highness, our consort, has given away the one he left for us here.

The studio of the duchess was on the ground floor of the Palazzo di Coste at Mantua. For this studio Mantegna, Correggio, Perugino and Costa painted nine pictures. Leonardo did nothing. In 1504, however, he accepted the commission to paint an Infant Christ for Isabella (see note on plate 20, and fig. 52).

XI. A LETTER FROM FRA PIETRO DA NOVELLARA TO MARCHESA ISABELLA D'ESTE OF MANTUA, APRIL 8TH, 1501; CONCERNING "THE CARTOON OF ST ANNE".

Leonardo's life is changeful and uncertain; it is thought that he lives only for the day. Since he has been in Florence, he has worked just on one cartoon, which represents an infant Christ of about one year, freeing himself almost out of his mother's arms and seizing a lamb and apparently about to embrace it. The mother half rising from the lap of St Anne is catching the child to draw it away from the lamb, that sacrificial animal which signifies the Passion. St Anne, just rising from her seat, as if she would wish to hinder her daughter from parting the Child from the lamb; which perhaps signifies the Church that would not wish the Passion of Christ to be hindered. The figures are life-size, but they fill only a small cartoon, because all are seated or bent, and each one is placed before the other, to the left. The sketch is not yet complete. He has done nothing else, except that he now and then lends a hand to one or another of the portraits which his two assistants are painting. He is entirely wrapped up in geometry and has no patience for painting.

Compare Sir Kenneth Clark, Windsor Drawings, p. 81; and notes to our plates 22, 87, 88, 89. Novellara describes the first cartoon of St Anne.—Concerning his important remark on Leonardo's touching up portraits by his pupils, compare plates 28 and 31.

XII. A LETTER FROM FRA PIETRO DA NOVELLARA, TO MARCHESA ISABELLA D'ESTE OF MANTUA, 14 APRIL, 1501; CONCERNING "THE MADONNA OF THE YARN-WINDER".

I have this week heard, through his pupil Salai and other of his friends, of Leonardo the artist's decision, which led me to visit him on the Wednesday of Passion Week in order to assure myself that it was true. In brief, his mathematical experiments have made painting so distasteful to him that he cannot even bear to take up a brush. However, I tried all I could, using first every art in order to get him to accede to your highness's wishes; and when I saw that he seemed well-disposed to place himself under obligation to your Eminence, I frankly told him everything, and we came to the following understanding, viz.: that, if he should be able to release himself from his engagement with the King of France without thereby forfeiting that monarch's goodwill (which he hoped might be managed in, at the most, a month's time), he would serve your Eminence in preference to any one else in the world. In any case, however, he will at once paint the portrait and forward it to your Eminence, as the small picture which he had to execute for one Robertet, a favourite of the King of France, is now finished. I left two with him, in order to expedite matters. The little picture represents a Madonna seated, and at work with a spindle, while the Infant Christ, with one foot upon the basket of flax, holds it by the handle, and looks with wonder at four rays of light, which fall in the form of a cross, as if wishing for them. Smilingly, he grasps the spindle, which he seeks to withhold from his mother. Thus much I was able to fix with him. I preached my sermon yesterday. God grant that it may bring forth rich fruit, for the hearers were numerous. I commend myself to your Eminence.

FRATER PETRUS DE NUVOLARIA

Vice-General of the Carmelite Monks.

Florence, April 4th, 1501.

(See Burlington Magazine, XLIX, August 1926, pp. 61-68, Emil Möller, "The Madonna of the Yarn-winder", in the possession of the Duke of Buccleuch. This painting is perhaps a studio replica of the Robertet Madonna; another copy is in the collection of R. W. Redford in Montreal, Canada.)

XIII. A DECREE BY CESARE BORGIA, ISSUED FROM PAVIA, 1502.

To all those of our *locotenenti, castellani, officiali* and *subditi*, whom it may concern, we herewith charge and command them, that they everywhere and in every place give free entrance to our highly-esteemed court architect Leonardo da Vinci, the bearer of this, who has been commissioned by us to inspect the fortresses and strongholds of our states, and to make such alterations and improvements as he may think needful. Both he and his followers are to be received with hospitality, and every facility afforded him for personal inspection, for measurement and valuation, just as he may wish. For that purpose a band of men is to be placed at his disposal, which is to give him all the help that he may require. With reference to the state works already in course of completion, we desire that every engineer be prepared to further any undertaking which he may find necessary.

XIV. A LETTER FROM FRANCESCO PANDOLFINI, FLORENTINE AMBASSADOR AT THE FRENCH COURT, FROM BLOIS, 22 JANUARY, 1507.

Finding myself this morning in the presence of the most Christian King, his Majesty called me and said: "Your lords must render me a service. Write to them that I desire to make use of their painter, Master Leonardo, who is now at Milan, and that I wish him to do certain things for me. Do this in such a way that their lordships enjoin him to serve me promptly, and tell him not to depart from Milan before my arrival. He is a good master, and I desire certain things by his hand. Write to Florence at once, and in such a way as to obtain the desired result, and send me the letter." All this came from a little painting by his hand that has recently been brought here, and which is judged to be a very excellent work. In the course of conversation I asked his Majesty what works he desired from him, and he answered, "Certain small pictures of Our Lady and others, according as the idea occurs to me : perhaps I shall get him to paint my portrait."

XV. DRAFT OF A LETTER FROM LEONARDO TO THE DUKE OF NEMOURS, GIULIANO DE' MEDICI, THE BROTHER OF LEO X, C. 1514.

I was so greatly rejoiced, most Illustrious Lord, by the desired restoration of your health that it almost had the effect that my own health recovered. . . . . But I am extremely vexed that I have not been able completely to satisfy the wishes of your Excellency, by reason of the wickedness of that deceiver, for whom I left nothing undone which could be done for him by me and by which I might be of use to him ; and in the first place his allowances were paid to him before the time, which I believe he would willingly deny, if I had not the writing signed by myself and the interpreter. And I, seeing that he did not work for me unless he had no work to do for others, which he was very careful in soliciting, invited him to eat with me, and to work afterwards near me, because, besides saving of expense, he would acquire the Italian language. (He always promised, but would never do so.) And this I did also, because that young German who makes the mirrors, was there always in the workshop, and wanted to see and to know all that was being done there and made it known outside blaming what he did not understand and because he dined with those of the Pope's guard, and then they went out with guns killing birds among the ruins ; and this went on from after dinner till the evening ; and when I sent Lorenzo to urge him to work he said that he would not have so many masters over him, and that his work was for Your Excellency's Wardrobe ; and thus two months passed and so it went on ; and one day finding Gian Niccolo of the Wardrobe and asking whether the German had finished the work for your Magnificence, he told me this was not true, but only that he had given him two guns to clean. Afterwards, when I urged him further, he left the workshop and began to work in his room, and lost much time in making another pair of pincers and files and other tools with screws ; and there he worked at reels for twisting silk which he hid when any one of my people went in, and with a thousand oaths and mutterings, so that none of them would go there any more.

[Another draft:]

I was so greatly rejoiced, most Illustrious Lord, by the desired restoration of your health that my own illness left me. But I am greatly vexed at not having been able to completely satisfy your Excellency's wishes by reason of the wickedness of that German deceiver, for whom I left nothing undone by which I could have hoped to please him; and first I invited him to lodge and board with me, by which means I should constantly see the work he was doing and with greater ease correct his errors, while, besides this, he would learn the Italian tongue, by means of which he could with more ease talk without an interpreter ; first his moneys were always given him in advance of the time when due. Afterwards he wanted to have the models finished in wood, just as they were to be in iron, and wished to carry them away to his own country. But this I refused him, telling him that I would give him, in drawing, the breadth, length, height and form of what he had to do ; and so we remained in ill will.

The next thing was that he made himself another workshop, and pincers and tools in his room where he slept, and there he worked for others ; afterwards he went to dine with the Swiss of the guard, where there are idle fellows, in which he beat them all ; from here he went out and most times they went in two or three with guns, to shoot birds among the ruins, and this went on till evening.

At last I found how this master Giovanni the mirror-maker was he who had done it all, for two reasons : the first because he had said that my coming here had deprived him of the countenance and favour of Your Lordship which always. . . . The other is that he said that his iron-workers' rooms suited him for working at his mirrors, and this he gave proof ; for besides making him my enemy, he made him sell all he had and leave his workshop to him, where he works with a number of workmen making numerous mirrors to send to the fairs.

Written in Rome while Leonardo was living in the Belvedere of the Vatican.

XVI. THE VISIT OF THE CARDINAL LUIGI D'ARAGONA, PAID TO LEONARDO, ON 10 OCTOBER, 1517 ; TOLD BY HIS SECRETARY, ANTONIO DE' BEATIS.

On the 10th of October, 1517, Monsignor and the rest of us went to see, in one of the outlying parts of Amboise, Messer Leonardo Vinci the Florentine, a grey-beard of more than seventy years, the most eminent painter of our time, who showed to his Eminence the Cardinal three pictures ; one of a certain Florentine lady, painted from life, at the instance of the late Lord Giuliano de' Medici ; the other of the youthful St John the Baptist ; and the third of the Madonna and the Child in the lap of St Anne, the most perfect of them all. One cannot indeed expect any more good work from him, as a certain paralysis has crippled his right hand. But he has a pupil, a Milanese, who works well enough : and although Messer Leonardo can no longer paint with the sweetness which was peculiar to him, he can still design and instruct others. This gentleman has written a treatise on anatomy, showing by illustrations, members, muscles, nerves, veins, joints, intestines, and whatever else is to discuss in the bodies of men and women, in a way that has never yet been done by any one else. All this we have seen with our own eyes ; and he said that he had dissected more than thirty bodies, both of men and women of all ages. He has also written of the nature of water, and of divers machines, and of other matters, which he has set down in an endless number of volumes, all in the vulgar tongue, which, if they be published, will be profitable and delightful.

St Anne, see plate 87 ; St John, see plate 100. The portrait of "a certain Florentine lady" was most probably the Mona Lisa (plate 26). The "Milanese pupil" is Francesco Melzi.

XVII. LETTER FROM FRANCESCO MELZI TO THE BROTHERS OF LEONARDO, ABOUT THE DEATH OF THE MASTER.

To Ser Giuliano and his honoured brothers—

I believe that the death of your brother, Maestro Leonardo, has already been certified to you. He was to me the best of fathers, and it is impossible for me to express the grief that his death has caused me. Until the day when my body is laid under the ground, I shall experience perpetual sorrow, and not without reason, for he daily showed me the most devoted and warmest affection.

His loss is a grief to everyone, for it is not in the power of nature to reproduce another such man. May the Almighty accord him everlasting rest. He passed from the present life on the 2nd of May with all the sacraments of holy Mother Church, and well disposed to receive them. The reason that he was able to make a will, leaving his goods to whom he liked, was on account of his possessing a letter from the king exempting him *quod heredes supplicantis sint regnicolae*. Without such a letter he would not have been able to will away anything he possessed here, this being the custom of the country. Maestro Leonardo accordingly made his will, which I should have sent you sooner had I been able to confide it to a trustworthy person. I expect that one of my uncles who has been to see me will soon return to Milan. I will dispose of it in his hands, and he will faithfully remit it to you. Up to the present time I have not found other means of sending it. In so much as concerns your part in the will, Maestro Leonardo possessed in the [hospital of] Santa Maria Nuova, in the hands of the treasurer, four hundred gold crowns (*scudi di sole*) in notes which have been placed out at five per cent for the last six years counting from last October. He had also an estate at Fiesole that he wished to be distributed equally among you. There is nothing more concerning you in the will, and I will say no more except to offer you my most willing service. You will find me ready and anxious to do your will.

I recommend myself continually to you.

Given at Amboise, the 1st of June, 1519.

Please reply by the Gondi,

Tanquam fratri vestro,

Franciscus Meltius

LIST OF DATES

1452   *Birth of Leonardo.*
1469   Lorenzo de' Medici comes to power in Florence.
       Ser Piero da Vinci, Leonardo's father, moves with his family into Florence. Leonardo in Verrocchio's workshop (since 1467 ?)
1472   *Leonardo's name entered in the Red Book of the Painters of Florence.*
1473   *First dated drawing of Leonardo (plate 105).*
1476   *Leonardo accused of sodomy with a model, Jacopo Saltarelli.*
1478   *Commission for an altar-piece in the Palazzo Vecchio (never painted). Leonardo in Pistoja.*

Fig. 32. Leonardo: Drawing, dated 1478, pen and ink. Florence, Uffizi.

1478   *Drawing with note by Leonardo: ". . . bre 1478 inchominciai le 2 S. Vergine Marie. . ." (which means that Leonardo began two Madonna paintings or reliefs in autumn 1478). Underneath is a line of which half is torn off; we can just read, ". . . e choppa a Pistoia" (the meaning is probably that the one Madonna was begun in Florence, the other in Pistoja). (Fig. 32.)*
1481   *Commission for the High Altar of the Convent of San Donato: The Adoration (plate 72).*
       Leonardo "in casa propria", his own lodgings.
1482   *Leonardo leaves Florence, and arrives, either in this year or in 1483, at the Court of Ludovico Sforza, called Il Moro, in Milan.*
1483   *Contract for the Virgin of the Rocks (plate 83).*
       Leonardo begins the Sforza monument (plates 138-141).
1488   Death of Verrocchio.
1489   *Leonardo designs dresses for the Court on the occasion of the marriage of Gian Galeazzo Sforza, and other decorations, including even horse-trappings.*
1490   *The Sforza monument recommenced.*
       In Pavia with Francesco di Giorgio.
       Salai, a boy of ten, comes to Leonardo's workshop in Milan; he lives with him for twenty-five years.
1493   *Model of the Sforza monument exhibited.*
1494   The Medici expelled from Florence.
1495   *Leonardo working on the Last Supper (plate 93).*
1496   (January 31) At the house of Conte di Cajazzo at Milan, in the presence of the Duke, a play on *Danae*, by Baldassare Taccone, is performed. *Leonardo designed the scenery.* (Fig. 33.)
       Luca Pacioli, professor of mathematics, moves to Milan and becomes friends with Leonardo.
       Baldassare Castiglione, the "complete gentleman", moves from the Court of Mantua to the Court of Milan.
1498   Death of Savonarola.
       "*Last Supper*" *finished.*
1499   *A vineyard given to Leonardo by the Duke Ludovico (April).*
       The French occupy Milan under Trivulzio (October).
       Leonardo flees from Milan (December).

1500   *Leonardo in Mantua: draws the portrait of Isabella d' Este (February).*
       In Venice (March).
       In Florence (April).
1501   *The first (lost) cartoon of St Anne.*
1502   *Leonardo in the service of Cesare Borgia.*
       Louis XII in Milan, visited by Cesare Borgia.
1503   *Leonardo in Florence: begins Cartoon of the Battle of Anghiari (plates 129-136). Mona Lisa (plate 26).*
1504   *Leonardo—together with Botticelli, Cosimo Roselli, Piero di Cosimo and others—in a committee of artists appointed to decide the best position of Michelangelo's David.*
       He starts the painting of the Anghiari Battle in the Palazzo Vecchio at Florence.
       His father dies.
1506   *Leonardo summoned to Milan, by the governor, Charles d' Amboise, (May).*
1507   Death of Cesare Borgia.
       Louis XII, king of France, in Milan (May).
       Leonardo returns to Florence (September).
1508   *Leonardo helps the sculptor Rustici.*
       Again in Milan (July).
1509   Luca Pacioli's "*De Divina Proportione*", issued in Venice, with 60 illustrations after designs of Leonardo.
1511   *Leonardo works on the Trivulzio monument (plates 144-146).*
       He meets the anatomist Marc Antonio della Torre, who helps him with his researches.
1512   The restoration of the Medici.
1513   *Leonardo leaves Milan with Salai and Melzi (September).*
       In Florence (October).
       Death of Pope Julius II; Giovanni de' Medici, who takes the name of Leo X, succeeds him.
       Leonardo arrives in Rome (December); stays in the Belvedere of the Vatican.
       The antique marble group of "The Nile" found in Rome and brought to the Belvedere.
1514   *Leonardo visits Parma (September).*

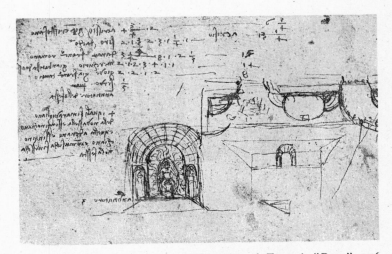

Fig. 33. Leonardo: Sketch for the stage setting of Taccone's "Danae", 1496. New York, Metropolitan Museum.

1515   Francis I, successor of Louis XII, recaptures Milan (October).   Francis I in Rome (December).
1516   Francis I returns to France (January).
       Leonardo notes measurements of San Paolo in Rome (August). Departs for France.
1517   *Leonardo in Amboise (May). Lives at the Manoir de Cloux, between the town and the Royal Castle.*
       The Cardinal Luigi d' Aragona visits Leonardo (October).
1519   *Death of Leonardo (2nd May).*

34    35    36

37    38    39 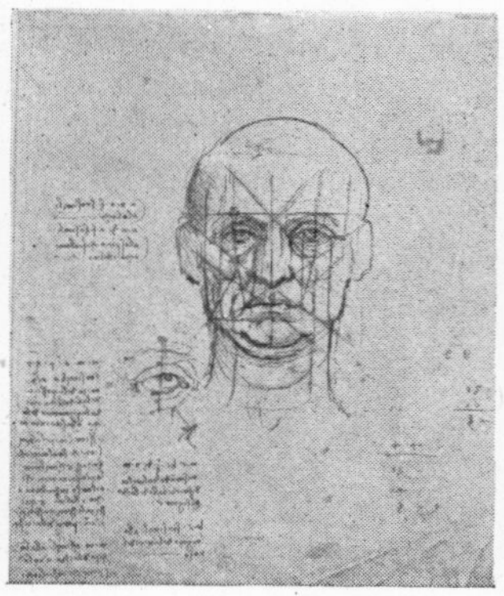   40    41

42    43    44    45

Figs. 34-45. *The appearance of Leonardo*—(34) Vasari's portrait of Leonardo, woodcut (detail), 1568.—(35) Portrait of Pietro da Navarra, c. 1510, by an unknown Florentine painter. Florence Uffizi.—(36) Portrait of Leonardo, c. 1498, red chalk drawing, perhaps by Ambrogio da Predis. Windsor, Royal Library.—(37) Supposed self-portrait of Leonardo, from the Adoration, cf. plate 72.—(38) Supposed portrait of Leonardo as St Michael, c. 1470-75. Detail from "Tobias and the Archangel", painted in Verrocchio's studio. Florence, Uffizi.—(39) Supposed portrait of Leonardo as David, c. 1468. Detail of a bronze figure by Verrocchio. Florence, Museo nazionale.—(40) Supposed self-portrait of Leonardo, c. 1496, pen and ink drawing, showing the proportions of the head. Turin, Royal Library.—(41) Study of an Apostle, supposed self-portrait of Leonardo, pen and ink, c. 1496. Amsterdam, Fodor Museum. — (42) Michelangelo : Pen and ink drawing, supposed portrait of Leonardo lecturing on anatomy, c. 1500. British Museum. — (43) Supposed portrait of Leonardo as Plato, detail from Raphael's School of Athens, 1509. Rome, Vatican.—(44) King David, detail from Raphael's Disputa del sacramento, 1509. Rome, Vatican.—(45) King Solomon, detail from Ghiberti's second bronze door of the Florentine Baptistery, c. 1450. (Type of the Sage in Florentine art, long before Leonardo's time).

NOTES ON THE PLATES

No. 1. SELF-PORTRAIT, TURIN, 1557¹

Repeatedly questioned as a self-portrait. According to Berenson (1083), retouched on nostrils and mouth.

Figs. 34-45 illustrate the different opinions held on the appearance of Leonardo. The profile of Vasari's woodcut (fig. 34) corresponds with the drawing at Windsor Castle (fig. 36), which shows Leonardo at a somewhat younger age. But the likeness, as given by Vasari, is very similar to the portrait of Pietro da Navarra (fig. 35), who in many ways was connected with Leonardo. First, he is called "inventor cuniculorum", inventor of underground passages or mines, a branch of war engineering in which Leonardo was also interested. Secondly, he was taken prisoner by the French after the battle at Ravenna, in 1512, and was afterwards in the service of Francis I, at the same time as Leonardo. It might well be that Pietro's portrait in Florence was based on a lost painting by Leonardo, and Vasari's woodcut erroneously executed from the same picture; but this is a question which cannot be discussed in a short note.

Berenson and Gronau thought they had found a youthful self-portrait of Leonardo in the "Adoration" (fig. 37); Müller-Walde and Bayersdorfer suspected that Leonardo was the model for the St Michael in Verrocchio's "Tobias" (fig. 38). But the "Tobias" is a doubtful work, and it would be easier to believe that Verrocchio's David bears the likeness of young Leonardo (fig. 39; hardly earlier than 1468). Beltrami contributed a little to the confusion by suggesting that certain sketches of heads (e.g. fig. 40) with measurements of proportions are self-portraits of Leonardo. Beltrami and Nicodemi maintain that the sketch of an Apostle in Amsterdam (fig. 41) is simply another self-portrait of the master, an idea which is no more persuasive than the old one connected with a drawing at Windsor (plate 16), once believed by Marie Herzfeld and Müntz to be a self-portrait. Möller suggested that a drawing by Michelangelo (fig. 42) was a portrait of Leonardo as anatomist, with a skull in his hand. This figure certainly reminds one of the Plato in Raphael's fresco, a portrait of Leonardo, at least by tradition (fig. 43). But even Raphael's representation is doubtful—or is it more Leonardo-like than his David (fig. 44)?

The type, anyway, is rather common in Florentine art at least, and only the early date of Ghiberti's "King Solomon" saves it from being taken for another Leonardo likeness (fig. 45).

I never doubted the Turin self-portrait, and I never felt at ease with any of the recent suggestions. I think I was the first to give a *late* date to the drawing—in my book on Self-Portraits.

No. 2. PORTRAIT OF FRANCESCO NANI, VICTORIA AND ALBERT MUSEUM

Page of a little bound note-book, marked SKM II-1, fol. 19A. Identification of the sitter by A. Popp (*Zeitschr. f. bildende Kunst*, LIX, 1925, p. 64). Nani helped Leonardo to get the commission for an altar-piece in the church of the Franciscans in Brescia, which he never executed (cf. Richter, § 679).

No. 3. PORTRAIT OF A MAN, WINDSOR, 12498

In a list of drawings, which Leonardo made c. 1482, one is named "A head of the Duke" (Richter, § 680). I always thought that Leonardo passed through Mantua, in 1482, on his way to Milan; he certainly did so in 1500, when he fled from Milan to Venice and back to Florence. If Leonardo came to Mantua in 1482, he must have met Marquis Federico Gonzaga, who reigned from 1478-84, and he saw the two frescoes in which Mantegna had portrayed Federico—the family group of Marquis Lodovico Gonzaga, in the Camera degli Sposi, c. 1470, and the other fresco in the same room of the castle, "The Meeting of Marquis Lodovico and Cardinal Francesco Gonzaga", c. 1473. From the latter fresco I reproduce here a detail, the portrait of Federico, which shows him at the age of thirty-three (fig. 46); I believe that Leonardo's drawing gives the likeness of the Duke when he was forty-two, overburdened by grief and already near his death.

No. 4. PORTRAIT OF CESARE BORGIA, TURIN, 15573

This drawing was formerly called "Oriental Heads"; the identification is by Valentiner and was accepted by Sir Kenneth Clark. (Cf. fig. 47.)

Fig. 46. Mantegna: Marquis Federico Gonzaga, c. 1473, from the "Meeting", in the Camera degli Sposi, Castello di Corte, Mantua. (Compare pl. 3)

Fig. 47. Cesare Borgia, portrait by an anonymous painter Florence, Uffizi. (Compare pl. 4)

No. 5. BUST OF A WARRIOR, BRITISH MUSEUM, 1895-9-15-474, from Malcolm Collection

Doubted by Morelli and others, and ascribed to Verrocchio. This drawing is done with the left hand, and it is certainly by Leonardo. It was always thought to be connected with two lost bronze reliefs, "Scipio" (or Alexander) and "Darius", executed in Verrocchio's workshop and sent to Matthias Corvinus of Hungary. Of those two reliefs, as Bode contended, old copies are preserved (*Leonardo-Studien*, p. 28); amongst others the Scipio relief in the Louvre from the Rattier collection (No. 668), which is sometimes attributed to Leonardo himself; and a clay relief of an old warrior in the Berlin Museum, attributed to the Robbia workshop (No. 2014. Sch. 188). The assumption is that Leonardo's drawing of an old warrior is freely copied from Verrocchio's Darius relief.

Leonardo's warrior is obviously a similar ideal type to Verrocchio's Colleoni (see figs. 48 and 49), and to the warrior in Verrocchio's silver relief of the "Beheading of the Baptist", from the altar of San Giovanni (now in the Museo del Duomo, Florence; reproduced Cruttwell, Verrocchio, pl. XXXIX). But all this only means that Leonardo was under the influence of his teacher at this early period, and it does not prove that he collaborated in any of the sculptures mentioned above.

More interesting is the fantastic armour of Leonardo's warrior, the armour *alla romana*. Armour of this kind was certainly produced in Verrocchio's workshop, and a helmet in the Florence Bargello shows the same bat wings, and the same circular ornaments on the wings (fig. 50). A Leonardo drawing at Windsor (12370) contains sketches for a highly decorated cuirass, proving how much Leonardo was interested in the armourer's art during the time he assisted Verrocchio.

Fig. 50. Florentine parade helmet, c. 1470. Florence, Bargello (*Armour "alla romana"—same as in fig. 48*).

Fig. 48. Detail from Leonardo's drawing of a Warrior, c. 1475. (Cf. pl. 5.)   Fig. 49. Detail from Verrocchio's Colleoni, 1479-88. Venice.

Nos. 6 and 7. HEADS OF WARRIORS, BUDAPEST

For the "Battle of Anghiari". Compare No. 132, and fig. 18.

No. 8. HEADS OF GIRLS AND MEN, WINDSOR 12276 v.

Recto of the same sheet contains the Madonna drawing, plate 63. The youth in the middle closely resembles the Rattier Relief, as Bode observed (cf. note on No. 5). The type of the old man was repeated by Leonardo throughout all his life.

No. 9. FIVE GROTESQUE HEADS, WINDSOR 12495

Sometimes called "The temperaments". The inscription on the reverse of the drawing, Richter § 1355. Sir Kenneth Clark: "This is the most important of all Leonardo's caricature drawings." Old copies in the Louvre and at Weimar.

No. 10. CARICATURE, WINDSOR, 12490

The figure at the right is a female.

No. 11. CARICATURE, WINDSOR, 12555v.

On the reverse a red chalk tracing and an inscription.

No. 12. HEAD OF A WARRIOR, VENICE 232

For the "Battle of Anghiari". Compare No. 7.

No. 13. OLD MAN AND YOUTH, UFFIZI, 423

Not very well preserved and partially retouched.

No. 14. CARICATURE, VENICE, 123

I have reproduced this small sheet on an enlarged scale to show the vehemence and the force of the pen strokes. The lines below are the rough sketch for some machine.

No. 15. BALDHEADED OLD MAN, WINDSOR, 12500

This physiognomical study, still containing some of the elements of Leonardo's caricature drawing, is so full of expression and pathos that we easily accept it as one of his most beautiful drawings.

No. 16. OLD MAN THINKING, WINDSOR, 12579

The sheet is folded in the middle, and contains two different drawings: the reproduction gives only the left half of the sheet. The right half shows sketches of swirling water and plaited hair, and a note (Richter § 389).

No. 17. STUDY FOR ST JAMES THE GREAT IN THE LAST SUPPER, WINDSOR, 12552

Compare plate 93, and 96; in No. 96 St James is in the middle.

No. 18. STUDY FOR ST BARTHOLOMEW IN THE LAST SUPPER, WINDSOR, 12548

Compare plate 93, and 95. Berenson thought it to be a study for the St Matthew, who is the third from the right in plate 93.

No. 19. STUDY FOR ST PHILIP IN THE LAST SUPPER, WINDSOR, 12551

Compare plate 93, and 96.

Fig. 51. Marco d'Oggiono: Christ bearing Fig. 52. Bernadino Luini: Christ in the Temple. (After Leonardo?) Fig. 53. Christ in the Temple, drawing by Hans Hoffmann (died 1592),
the globe. Rome, Villa Borghese. London, National Gallery. after a cartoon by Dürer (?) Budapest, Museum of Fine Arts.

No. 20. STUDY FOR THE HEAD OF A PHARISEE, WINDSOR, 19106

Seidlitz thought (1) it a study for the Judas in the Last Supper (second edition, p. 150 and ill. 87). The sheet is folded in the middle, the left half containing little sketches of twigs and notes on physics; the right half (which alone is reproduced here) the turbanned head. Sir Kenneth Clark connects this drawing with a (lost) painting, Christ in the Temple, for which Leonardo received a commission, in 1504, from Isabella d'Este of Mantua. Clark explained that Leonardo twice painted the youthful Jesus for Isabella (Windsor, note on No. 12524, and Leonardo, p. 129); once as Christ bearing the globe, and once as Christ among the Doctors, and he pointed out that several copies, derived from Leonardo's compositions, are extant. A copy of the globe-bearing Christ is reproduced here, fig. 51; of the Christ in the Temple, fig. 52; and lastly, fig. 53, the same composition in a northern idiom by Hans Hoffmann, who made use of Dürer's painting of 1506 (now in the Palazzo Barberini, Rome) but much more Leonardesque. (Cf. G. Glück, in *Jahrb. d. Kunsthist. Samml. Wien*, XXVIII, p. 8.)

Fig. 54. Lorenzo di Credi: The Lady of the Juniper, c. 1478. New York.
Richard de Wolfe Brixey Collection.

No. 21. ST PETER, ALBERTINA, VIENNA

The drawing was originally in silverpoint; the pen and ink are by a later hand. The study was not used in the Last Supper— see the fifth figure from the left on plate 93.

No. 22. ST ANNE, WINDSOR, 12534

Study for the *first* cartoon of St Anne; see Documents XI, p. 21. The face in the drawing much retouched by a later hand.

No. 23. PORTRAIT OF GINEVRA DE' BENCI, VIENNA, LIECHTENSTEIN GALLERY, 38

On the reverse a sprig of juniper encircled by laurel and palm, forming a garland, with the inscription *"virtutem forma decorat"*. The garland, in its mutilated shape, on the back of the panel proves that the painting has been cut by c. 8 inches; the lower part, originally containing the hands, is lost. The slit of the bodice has been overpainted; originally the fingers of the right hand, probably holding some flowers, were painted here. A drawing at Windsor (reproduced here as No. 40) might have been a study for the hands of this portrait; or we may compare the hands of the Lady with Primroses (No. 148) in order to visualize the portrait as it was before it was cut. (2)

Juniper (*ginepro* or *ginevra* in Italian) is the symbol for the name of the sitter. The author of the *libro Billi* (c. 1515), the Anonimo Gaddiano (c. 1540) and Vasari (1550 and 1568) confirm that Leonardo portrayed Ginevra de' Benci, and they praise the picture. The Anonimo says: *"Ritrasse in Firenze al naturale la Ginevra d'Amerigo Benci, la quale tanto bene finì, che non il ritratto ma la propria Ginevra pareva."* Waagen, 1866, was the first to identify the Liechtenstein painting with Leonardo's Ginevra portrait; but until 1939 it was usually attributed to Lorenzo di Credi. A portrait in a private collection at New York, one of the best Credi ever painted and apparently inspired by the Liechtenstein panel (fig.54), exemplifies the difference in quality between the two pupils of Verrocchio.

No. 24. PORTRAIT OF ISABELLA D'ESTE, LOUVRE, M.I. 753

The drawing is pricked for transfer, but the painting done from it is lost. Leonardo painted Isabella in 1500—see Documents IX and X. There were at least two portraits, one which Leonardo left in Mantua (and which probably was later in Fontainebleau) and one which he had with him in Venice, as we know from a letter from the Ambassador of Mantua to Isabella, dated 13th March, 1500. And it may be that Leonardo painted a third "sketch", fulfilling Isabella's wish.

The cartoon reproduced here is of very poor preservation. The reproduction gives only a part of the drawing, as the head only is by Leonardo, and the dress and the hand by a mediocre pupil,

---

(1) *This view could be defended from the standpoint of technique; Leonardo hardly used wash after 1490.*

(2) *Why has the lower part of the painting been cut off? No one painted hands more beautifully than Leonardo did. I suspect that the painting was unfinished, the hands only sketched in (as the left hand of the Lady with the Ermine, or the right hand of the Musician, plates 29 and 30). Ginevra was born in 1456, in 1473 she married Luigi Niccolini, in 1490 she was still alive. At about this time Domenico Ghirlandaio painted her profile, in "The Visitation", a mural in Santa Maria Novella at Florence (Photo Alinari, 4594).*

who unfortunately was bold enough to redraw even the profile. The cartoon must have been famous, because there are several old copies of it, including one at Oxford, showing the hands in the right position resting on a book, and one at the Uffizi, the head only, probably by Ambrogio da Predis.

A red chalk drawing at Florence (Uffizi, 419) has been wrongly identified with Leonardo's Isabella portrait. (First by Allessandro Luzio, *Galleria dei Gonzaga*, Milan 1913, opp. pag. 144, "*Il vero rittrato Leonardesco d' Isabella*". In the Leonardo Exhibition, Milan 1939, it was also shown as Leonardo's Portrait of Isabella d'Este.) The drawing was formerly attributed to Franciabigio, Bacchiacca and Pontormo, and is, as I think, a portrait of Bandinelli's wife (see figs. 55 and 56).

Fig. 55. Baccio Bandinelli : Portrait of his wife, c. 1515. Florence, Uffizi.   Fig. 56. Baccio Bandinelli : Portrait of his wife, c. 1525. Paris, Louvre.

No. 25. PORTRAIT OF A GIRL, WINDSOR, 12505

Chin and other parts re-drawn, but apparently by Leonardo himself.—For a similar profile see plate 8.

Nos. 26-27. MONA LISA, LOUVRE, No. 1601

The only Leonardo portrait painting which has never been questioned. The sitter was Lisa Gherardini, born 1479, married in 1495 to Francesco di Zanobi del Giocondo of Florence. Valentiner suggested that the portrait was not painted for the husband but for Giuliano de' Medici, alleged lover of Mona Lisa. Leonardo brought the painting to France (see Document XVI), where Francis the First bought it for 12.000 francs.

The preservation of the painting is not too good ; there are overpaintings in the dress, the veil, the right hand, in the sky and elsewhere. Part of the glazes is rubbed off, and the whole is covered by dirty greenish varnish. The picture is cut both sides, about 3 inches.

The cleaning of the picture has often been considered, but the French artists, especially Degas, protested against it ; and they were probably right.

Many pages have been written since Vasari's time on the "Smile of the Gioconda". A Frenchman (Robert de Sizeranne, 1896) has observed that Gioconda smiles with only the left part of her mouth —but this is in accordance with the advice given to women in Renaissance times as to how to look most graceful : we read in Agnolo Firenzuola's "*Della perfetta bellezza d'una donna*," 1541 : "From time to time, to close the mouth at the right corner with a suave and nimble movement, and to open it at the left side, as if you were smiling secretly. . . . not in an artificial manner, but as though unconsciously—this is not affectation, if it is done in moderation and in a restrained and graceful manner and accompanied by innocent coquetry and by certain movements of the eyes. . . ." This is a precept for ladies of fashion, and we should not overlook the fact that Mona Lisa—who plucked her eye-brows and the hair above her brow—was one of them.

[This portrait is probably the most popular painting in the world. And its popularity was considerably enhanced when thirty years ago it was stolen from the Louvre and remained undiscovered for more than two years. The thief was an Italian house-painter, Vincenzo Peruggia, who did occasional work at the Louvre. On the 21st of August, 1911, at 8 o'clock in the morning, he took the picture out of its frame, put it under his workman's blouse, marched through a backdoor and down to the quay. He was questioned by the Police, but they did not find the painting which he kept in a small store-room at his lodgings. When two years later, in

Florence, Mr Peruggia offered the smiling Giocondo to an art-dealer, Alfred Gori by name, he was arrested, and the picture was surrendered to the French Ambassador on the 21st December, 1913. Mr Peruggia declared he had taken this Italian picture to Italy, being himself a Lombard and a patriot. He did not mention Napoleon, who had snatched away from Italy so many works of art which one can now see in the Louvre—and he was sentenced to seven months imprisonment.]

No. 28. "LA BELLE FERRONNIÈRE", LOUVRE, No. 1600

The lady wears a small *scuffia*, or cap, on the back of her head, and a *ferronnière* round her brow. (A *ferronnière* is a head-band which originally formed the velvet rim of a hair net, but was later made of gold and ornamented with jewels.) This was a common Lombard fashion.

The portrait of "A Lady with a Ferronière" was at one time confused with La Belle Ferronnière, who was a mistress of Francis I.

Claiming it in 1839 as a portrait of Lucrezia Crivelli, Waagen was the first to attribute it to Leonardo. In 1894 Frizzoni was the first to attribute it to Boltraffio. In our time some of the best authorities—including A. Venturi, Berenson, Sir Charles Holmes, and Beltrami—have reverted to belief in Leonardo's authorship.

We recall a letter, written by Pietro da Novellara in 1501 (Documents, XI) in which he says : "Leonardo has done nothing else, except that he now and then lends a hand to one or another of the portraits which his two assistants are painting." Boltraffio, born in 1467, joined Leonardo's studio not later than 1490 ; the portrait of the Lady with the *ferronnière* must be dated somewhat earlier, as it closely resembles in style the two autograph Leonardo paintings, The Lady with an Ermine, and The Musician (plates 29 and 30). I follow Suida in detecting here a joint work of Boltraffio and his master.

No. 29. LADY WITH AN ERMINE, CRACOW, No. 180

In ancient times Ermines (Greek, *galé*) were kept as mouse-hunters instead of cats(1). This also appears to have been sometimes a custom in the Renaissance, as a big weasel is depicted in this portrait, and a small one in a lady's portrait from Titian's studio (Vienna Museum, and a variant in the John Ringling Art Museum, Sarasota, U.S.A.).

Leonardo used the ermine, or *galé*, as a speaking symbol in this portrait of Cecilia Gallerani, as he used the juniper, or ginevra, in the portrait of Ginevra de' Benci ; a cock, or *gallo*, in the allegory on Gian Galeazzo Sforza ; and the knots, the *fantasie dei vinci*, as a symbol for his own name.

Cecilia Gallerani became the mistress of Ludovico Moro in 1481 and the portrait was painted shortly after Leonardo arrived in Milan.

The ermine is the best part of the picture, as the experts, including Ochenkowski, Hildebrandt and Clark, are all agreed. Otherwise, the painting is not well preserved.

The lower part of the hand has been repainted as well as the left shoulder and the part of the dress underneath the ermine, where Cecilia's right hand was originally sketched in. The dark background is new, and the outline of the figure spoilt by it. New also is the inscription in the upper left corner : "La belle Feroniere Leonard d'Awinci," which suggests that the picture had been in France before it came into the possession of Prince Adam Czartoryski during the French Revolution.

In spite of its doubtful preservation, this is Leonardo's most charming portrait painting.

No. 30. PORTRAIT OF A MUSICIAN, AMBROSIANA, sala D, 19

In Leonardo's List of Drawings (Richter § 680) of c. 1482 there is one item : "*una testa ritratta d'Atalanta che alzava il volto.*" This probably means that Leonardo portrayed the musician Atalanta

---

(1) "*Professor Rolleston and others believed that the domestic animal of the Greeks and Romans, for which we now use the cat, was the white-breasted marten. The word* feles, *it is true, is commonly used for the weasel.*" (*Watkins, Natural History of the Ancients, London, 1896, p. 63). Bode (Leonardo-Studien, p. 112) thought that Leonardo was depicting a marten, or rather a ferret (Mustela furo), as he never saw a real ermine. (See also G. Jennison, Animals in Ancient Rome, 1937, pp. 19 and 129.)*

MONA LISA (CF. PL. 26)

Migliorotti, who had learned from him to play the lyra (according to the Anonimo Gaddiano) and who went with him from Florence to Milan in 1492. Atalanta was born in 1466—the Ambrosiana musician might be a man of twenty—, in 1490 he went to Mantua; and in 1513, when Leonardo went to Rome, he found Atalanta there as Superintendent of the buildings of Pope Leo X.

Nevertheless, Luca Beltrami, who saw in the Ambrosiana picture a portrait of Franchino Gaffurio, was probably right. In 1905, the picture was freed from overpaint, and the sheet was revealed with music notes and a half-effaced inscription line on it, reading CANT . . . ANG . . . Now Gaffurio, conductor of the Cathedral choir in Milan from 1482, was the author of an "Angelicum ac divinum opus," not published until 1508, but composed probably much earlier. I read the inscription on the sheet in the Ambrosiana musician's hand as "canticum angelicum," and I think it is the title of a work by Gaffurio. According to Gerolamo Adda, Leonardo made the designs for the woodcuts in Gaffurio's "Practica musica," published 1496. Gaffurio was of about the same age as Leonardo.

This portrait is the only painting by Leonardo(1) which is in a perfect state of preservation. Only the face and a part of the hair is finished; everything else, including the hand, is just sketched in. All the brush strokes, especially those on the cheek-bone and the neck, seem to me to be made by a left-handed painter. For the rather strange design of the eyes, compare the drawing of an angel, from the same period of Leonardo, plate 35.

No. 31. PORTRAIT OF A YOUNG LADY IN PROFILE, AMBROSIANA, sala E, 8

Müller-Walde thought it a portrait of Bianca, a natural daughter of Ludovico Moro, for which painting Leonardo received a commission in 1491. Bode, Gronau and Beltrami attributed it without any reservation to Leonardo; Suida thinks that Leonardo did the better part of the portrait; Sir Kenneth Clark believes that the master may have painted some of the details, especially the head-dress(2). But Morelli, Berenson, Bodmer, Sirén and other experts regard it as the master-piece of Ambrogio da Predis.

I believe that it was designed by Leonardo but not executed by him. Ambrogio da Predis is certainly responsible for some of the weaknesses of the painting, mainly for the pitch-dark background, by which he even spoiled the outlines of the back of the head and the shoulder. The flesh is much better modelled, softer and more lifelike than anything Predis ever painted, including the Archinto portrait with its sooty shadows in the National Gallery, dated 1494, or the utterly disagreeable profile of Maximilian in the Vienna Museum, dated 1502.

There is only one profile portrait of similar quality, done by a pupil of Leonardo, the head of Girolamo Casio, in Boltraffio's "Madonna of the Casio family", painted in 1500, (Louvre, No. 1169).

Profile portraits by Leonardo are scarce; but compare, for example, plate 25; or figure 13, the portrait of Beatrice d'Este, which both belong to the 1490's. Was Müller-Walde right to date the Ambrosiana profile portrait of a lady, 1491?

---

(1) *It is only during the last ten years or so that the majority of experts have agreed in ascribing this masterpiece to Leonardo and not to second-rate painters such as Ambrogio da Predis. But it must be remembered that very queer opinions were once held about Leonardo as a portraitist, and a hundred years ago he was even confused with Holbein!*
Holbein's portrait of Morette in the Dresden Gallery was thought to be a portrait of Ludovico Moro by Leonardo; and in William Hazlitt's "Sketches of the Picture Galleries of England" (second edition, 1843, p. 69) we read about a painting at Windsor Castle: "A Head, said to be by Leonardo da Vinci—but more like Holbein." On the other hand the criticism of the last generation since Morelli went too far: we ought to be glad that the three important portraits—the Musician, the Lady with the Ermine, and the Lady of the Juniper—have been given back to Leonardo.

(2) *May we assume that Leonardo designed, for the Court jeweller, jewellery as worn by the Lady of this portrait? The golden ghirlanda or ferronnière round the brow, the net made of gold wire and pearls, and the interlaced wire ornament over the shoulder are of exquisite design. An engraving by Jaques Prévost de Gray, a portrait of Francis I (Bibl. Nat. Paris, reprod. Bouchot, Pièces choisies de l'école Française), shows the King with a neck-chain formed of shells and fantasie dei vinci, which looks as if designed by Leonardo.*

No. 32. STUDY FOR THE HEAD OF LEDA, WINDSOR, 12518

Leonardo made two different cartoons for a Leda painting, one for a Leda with the Swan in a crouching position, and one for a standing Leda. (Cf. note on No. 56.) The latter was copied by Raphael during his stay at Florence, c. 1506, in a pen and ink drawing which is now in the Windsor Castle Library.

A sketch in oil, from Leonardo's studio, of a similar head, is in Lord Melchett's possession (fig. 57).

Fig. 57. Head of Leda, c. 1510-13. Romsey, Lord Melchett.

No. 33. STUDY FOR THE HEAD OF LEDA, WINDSOR, 12516

Cf. notes on No. 32 and 56. Popp and Clark date c. 1510.

No. 34. STUDY FOR THE HEAD OF ST ANNE, WINDSOR, 12533   Cf. No. 87.

No. 35. STUDY FOR THE ANGEL'S HEAD IN THE VIRGIN OF THE ROCKS, TURIN, 15572

Cf. plates 83 and 86.

No. 36. DRAPERY OF A PRAYING MADONNA, PALAZZO CORSINI, 125770

Compare note 9 of the "Life" by Vasari (p. 6 of this book). Popp connected this drawing with the Louvre Annunciation (fig. 24) pointing out that it was not used for the Madonna but for the angel, in a reversed way, as seen in a mirror.

No. 36-A. DRAPERY FOR A KNEELING FIGURE, WINDSOR, 12521 (Frontispiece)

Seidlitz and Popham connected the drawing with Verrocchio's Baptism of Christ (figs. 5 and 6), Venturi with the Annunciation (plate 66), Sir Kenneth Clark with the Madonna of the Rocks in the National Gallery (plate 84). I cannot see that Leonardo used this drapery study in any of his paintings; it was probably done for an Adoration of the Child—compare plate 81.

No. 37. DRAPERY STUDY IN BLACK AND WHITE ON LINEN, FLORENCE, UFFIZI

See Clark's "Leonardo", page 12, note 1, where a list of genuine drapery studies on linen is given: one in the British Museum, three in the Louvre, five in the Collection of Mme. la Comtesse de Behague, and three in the Uffizi.

Nos. 38 and 39. DRAPERY STUDIES FOR THE MADONNA IN THE ST ANNE PAINTING, WINDSOR, 12532 and 12530

Compare plate 87

No. 40. STUDY OF A WOMAN'S HANDS, WINDSOR, 12558

See the notes on the plates 23 and 148 : the drawing has been connected with the Ginevra portrait in the Liechtenstein Gallery, and with the Marble bust of a Lady with Primroses (pl. 23, 148).

Nos. 41 and 42. NUDE FIGURE OF A MAN, FACING THE SPECTATOR, AND BACK TURNED TO THE SPECTATOR, WINDSOR, 12594 and 12596

Probably done in connection with the earliest studies for the Battle of Anghiari ; cf. plate 46.

No. 43. STUDIES FOR ST JOHN, WINDSOR, 12540

The sketch of the Infant St John is related to the same figure in two compositions which were attributed to Cesare da Sesto : the Vierge aux Balances in the Louvre, and the Madonna Harris, otherwise called The Madonna with the playing Children ; but the position of the limbs is different. The Infant Christ of The Madonna with the Lamb (Brera No. 286, ascribed to Sodoma) is rather similar. I cannot see any connection between this sketch and the first St Anne Cartoon.

The seated youthful St John recalls indeed the St John in the Desert, or Bacchus (Louvre, No. 1602), which has been ascribed to Cesare da Sesto and Bernazzone, a composition of which Leonardo is certainly innocent.

(Compare also the pen and ink drawing at Weimar, reprod. Seidlitz, first edition, vol. I, p. 80).

No. 44. STUDIES OF THE MOVEMENTS OF THE HUMAN FIGURE, WINDSOR, 1264

The lower part of the sheet, which is blank, is not reproduced. The movements of the two nude youths remind one of the St John in plate 43, or—as Sir Kenneth Clark found—of "the attitude of one of Michelangelo's athletes" in the Sistine ceiling fresco. The figure below represents a woman lowering a bucket into the water.

No. 45. A MAN CLIMBING A LADDER, VICTORIA AND ALBERT MUSEUM

Page of a little bound note-book, marked SKM II-1, fol. 45B. For the text, of which the last five lines are in black ink, see Richter § 376.

No. 46. FIGURE STUDIES FOR THE BATTLE OF ANGHIARI, TURIN, 15577

From left to right : nude woman in the attitude of the standing Leda with the swan ; nude woman with child ; nude soldier with sword, his back turned to the spectator ; same figure with arms raised and muscles more pronounced.

Below : four studies of a foot-soldier ; galloping horseman (cf. pl. 131 and 134, upper left part) ; rider on pacing horse ; galloping horse (cf. e.g. plate 147).

No. 47. MEASURED HEAD AND HORSEMEN, VENICE, 236

Head in ink over black chalk, with measurements ; and text, Richter § 315. Richter dates the writing "earlier than 1480" ; Sir Kenneth Clark (note on Windsor drawing No. 12340) "without question, c. 1490." The latter date is given by Popp to the whole drawing, but we follow Berenson, Bodmer and Clark in believing that the remaining part of the drawing, viz., the two horsemen in red chalk, belong to a later period, i.e., when Leonardo was working on the Anghiari battle cartoon, c. 1504 (cf. pl. 131). Popp said that the figure on horseback on the left was an Amazon.

No. 48. THE PROPORTIONS OF THE HUMAN FIGURE, VENICE, 228

This drawing is an illustration to a passage in Vitruvius, book III, cap. 1 (Richter § 343), and Leonardo's writing on the sheet is a free rendering of what Vitruvius said ; but Leonardo did not copy the sentences which he in fact illustrated, viz. : "The navel is naturally placed in the centre of the human body, and if a circle be described of a man lying with his face upward and his hands and feet extended, it will touch his fingers and his toes. It is not alone by a circle that the human body is thus circumscribed, as may be seen by placing it within a square. For if we measure from the feet to the crown of the head, and then across the arms fully extended, we should find the latter measure equal to the former ; so that the lines at right angles to each other enclosing the figure, would form a square."

No. 49. HALF-FIGURE OF A WOMAN, WINDSOR, 12508

Drawn probably during Leonardo's stay in Rome ; his closest approach to Hellenistic art.

No. 50. DANCING MAIDENS, VENICE, 233

The draperies of the maidens remind one of the angels in Botticelli's Nativity, 1500, in the National Gallery, but still more of the dancing muses in Mantegna's Parnassus, 1497 (Louvre, No. 1375), once in the boudoir of Isabella d'Este at Mantua. Was Leonardo influenced by Mantegna, or were he and the other painters inspired by the Hellenistic relief of the Horae ? Figs. 58 and 59 show how this classical motive was used in the schools of Florence and Padua. (Cf. Euripides Ion, 495-98 : " Where the maidens three to Agraulus born tread with their feet the dance over the grassy lawn before Athena's shrine.")

No. 51. A NYMPH, WINDSOR, 12581

This drawing, probably done during Leonardo's late period in Rome and under the influence of Hellenistic reliefs, also shows how far Leonardo had returned to the style of his native Florence.

The landscape—with the little waterfall in the left corner, the trees on both sides, the river, and the hills disappearing in the distance as in a grey haze—is barely indicated, but is as full of atmosphere as any late drawing by Rembrandt.

Fig. 58. Domenico Ghirlandajo: Dancing Maidens, pen and ink drawing. c. 1490. Stockholm, National Museum.

Fig. 59. Zoan Andrea : The dancing muses, engraving after Mantegna's Parnassus, 1497. London, British Museum (B. XIII. 305).

No. 52. YOUTH IN MASQUERADE COSTUME,
WINDSOR, 12575

Malaguzzi Valeri, Seidlitz and Bodmer dated this drawing early, connecting it with a masquerade for Galeazzo di Sanseverino, in 1491; Müller-Walde thought it was done in the first Florentine period, for the joust of Giuliano de' Medici in 1475. Calvi attributed it to the later Milan period. Popp believed it was even later than drawings like pl. 145, and attributed it to the French period, 1516-18. Sir Kenneth Clark thought the drawing should be dated after 1512. Thus, the main problem of this drawing is its date.

In May, 1506, Leonardo was summoned to Milan by the Governor, Charles d'Amboise; he obtained three months leave from the Signoria of Florence, and in September of that year the leave was prolonged, without the Signoria's consent. One year later, Leonardo was again in Florence for a short stay. In 1506 he had suspended his work on the painting of the Battle of Anghiari in the Sala di Gran Consiglio, and he never resumed it. Why was Leonardo summoned to Milan? The originally agreed term of leave of three months was not long enough to paint a picture, especially by Leonardo, who was known to require as many years, and certainly he would not have been granted leave merely to execute an altar-piece for an obscure monastery. I think this leave was granted because Louis XII was expected in Milan, who actually entered the town on the 23rd May, 1507, when three triumphal arches were erected in his honour and two hundred youths in costumes of blue silk welcomed him(1). I fancy Leonardo's masquerade drawings (Windsor, 12573-77) were done in this year.

All Leonardo's late drawings are marked by a profound *tristesse* —see plates 15, 16, 49-51, 106-112—and exhibit a dissolution of form which recall the later Titian and Rembrandt. I cannot discern the same spirit in those lively and plastic costume drawings which continue the style of the drawings for the St Anne cartoon (cf. pl. 89A), but are earlier than those for the Trivulzio monument (cf. pl. 144). As far as can be judged from the finished drawing, belonging to the same series of masquerade sketches, the young man on horseback (Windsor 12574) was originally a black chalk drawing not unlike the nude soldier in the Venice drawing, pl. 47, and the costume was later added in pen and ink. I should not date any of the Windsor drawings 12573-77 later than 1507.

No. 53. ALLEGORY OF THE LIZARD, METROPOLITAN
MUSEUM, NEW YORK

The whole sheet is 20,2 x 13,6 cm, but I have not reproduced the part which is blank. This drawing belongs to a series of illustrations by Leonardo to moralizing tales of animals— called "The Bestiary of Physiologus", a book which was compiled in Alexandria, c. 300 A.D., and of which many variations were composed and were popular during the Middle Ages. Most of Leonardo's Tales of Animals are in the Manuscript H-1, at the Institute of France in Paris, dating from March 1494; but the sheets of this note-book are much smaller than the sheet in New York. On the reverse of the drawing are the sketch for the scenery and the Dramatis Personae of a Danaë play, which was actually performed on January 31, 1496, at Milan (see fig. 33). Richter(2), therefore dated both sides of the sheet in New York, 1495. (Popp and Bodmer assumed without good reason an earlier date, c.1492-93 for the Allegory of the Lizard, and a later date for the reverse.) Translation of the text on this drawing: "The lizard is faithful to man, and when it sees that he is asleep it will fight the snake, and when it realizes that it cannot conquer it will run across the face of the man and wake him so that the snake should not hurt him while asleep."

No. 54. ALLEGORY, LOUVRE, 2247

This allegory was certainly designed for Ludovico Moro, because the sun has here the same shape as in the Duke's coat-of-arms; but the meaning of this allegory is not yet found. The youth reflects the sun in a bright shield or convex mirror; a dragon tries to kill a panther, a second panther is seen in the foreground; a bear is attacking the dragon, and from the left a unicorn is advancing to help; behind the rocks a boar is hiding.

The drawing is not a very early one but belongs to the same period as some of the emblems and allegories in Manuscript H, which is dated 1493-94 (cf. Richter § 694-696). On a sheet in the British Museum (Codex Arundel, 250a, datable 1499) there is among others, this sentence: "On the shield a large mirror to signify that he who truly desires favour must be mirrored in his virtues." The sun is a symbol of truth (cf. Richter § 684).

No. 55. ALLEGORY, CHRIST CHURCH LIBRARY,
OXFORD A.32 (Colvin I, 16)

Group of two women, seated on a cage: one woman holding a sword and a mirror in which the face of an old man is reflected. This face appears on the back of the head of the other woman, whereas the face turned to the right is the face of a lovely young girl. The two female figures symbolize Justice and Prudence. The double-faced Prudence swings a faggot which is encircled by a snake, the heraldic animal of the Sforzas. Snakes are also seen at the foot of the cage, attacking the hounds or wolves which are driven by a satyr. In the air are two birds of prey. In Manuscript H (Richter § 1249) there is this note by Leonardo: "The serpent is a very large animal. When it sees a bird in the air, it draws in its breath so strongly that it draws the birds into its mouth too." On the cage (not in the cage) is a cock (*gallo* in Italian; one Greek word for Cage is *galèdgra*), the symbol of Gian Galeazzo Sforza, the rightful heir to the throne of Milan, kept as a prisoner by his uncle Ludovico Moro, and poisoned by him (3) in 1494. The allegory seems to say that Galeazzo was not really a prisoner but kept safely by Ludovico's prudence and justice from enemies who otherwise would destroy him.

This drawing was probably done in 1484, when a conspiracy in favour of Galeazzo was detected and suppressed.

On the back of the drawing is a winged figure (seen reversed in plate 55 on the left) with a book as a shield and a writing point as a spear, pursuing a female figure, an archer who is marked "envy". The point of Envy's arrow is a human tongue. The winged figure is marked "Fama o Virtù". In the background are scribbles indicating two figures, one the Fama, blowing a trumpet, and the other a youth holding his ears(4).

---

(3) *On the 2nd of January, 1495, Florence sent two ambassadors to Milan to congratulate Ludovico Sforza on his becoming Duke of Milan; until the death of Galeazzo he was not called Duke.*

(4) *This trumpet-blowing figure resembles two early drawings by Leonardo, of c. 1482, in the British Museum (1886-6-9-42 recto, and 1895-9-15-478).*

Fig. 60. Bathing Venus. Marble, by Doidalsas of Bithynia, about 250 B.C. Louvre.

---

(1) *In Luca Landucci's Florentine Diary there is a note under the 23rd May, 1507: "The King of France entered Milan, and there were jousts and feasts."*   (2) *No. 43 of his List of Manuscripts.*

No. 56. LEDA AND THE SWAN, FRANZ KOENIGS
COLLECTION (formerly in the Grand Ducal Library
at Weimar)

Compare the notes on Nos. 32 and 33. A sketch in the Codex
Atlanticus (289 recto), datable c. 1503, two small sketches at
Windsor (12337, one reproduced as 56B), a doubtful drawing at
Chatsworth (reproduced as 56A), an unpleasing painting at Castle
Neuwied (usually ascribed to Gianpetrino)—that is all that is left
of Leonardo's composition of a kneeling Leda. The mother of
Castor and Pollux, of Clytemnestra and Helen, appears in this
drawing sharply differentiated from the slender Venus of Botti-
celli, the tall figure of Eve as the Florentines drew her since
Ghiberti, or even Raphael's Three Graces : it is a baroque type of
a woman, fleshy, like a mare : fertility symbolized by heavy curves.
This Leda is the re-born Bathing Venus of the Greek Baroque
(see fig. 60) and the forerunner of the fat beauties of Rubens.

No. 56A. LEDA, CHATSWORTH, 717

As far as I know, only Bodmer (p. 417) believes it to be an
autograph drawing. I think he is right—but some of the lines,
especially the right foreground, seem to be strengthened by a
later hand. Pen and ink over black chalk.

No. 56B. STUDY OF A LEDA, WINDSOR, 12337

This is a detail from a sheet which contains two more sketches
of a kneeling Leda, horses and horsemen, etc. In this version the
right arm of Leda is stretched across her body as in all the copies
of the standing Leda (see fig. 61). Cf. notes on Nos. 32, 33, 56.
Sketches for the Standing Leda—Windsor, 12642, and Codex
Atlanticus 156r.

Fig. 62. David, or Neptune. Detail of a pen and ink drawing by Leonardo, c. 1501-04. Windsor, Royal Library (12591r).

Fig. 63. Nude Youth, holding a staff. Pen and ink drawing by Leonardo, c. 1513. British Museum (1860-6-16-97).

No. 57. NEPTUNE, WINDSOR, 12570

A study for the cartoon which, according to Vasari, Leonardo
did for his "good friend Antonio Segni". The definite drawing
contained more figures, because Vasari mentions "sprites, dolphins
and winds, and several most beautiful heads of sea gods."
Raphael's "Triumph of Galatea", 1514, was probably influenced
by Leonardo's "Neptune and the Sea-gods" ; and how the "Winds"
looked we can imagine by comparing the upper left corner of
the Windsor drawing, plate 106.

The motif was perhaps taken from the antique, as, for instance,
a bronze plaquette in the Dreyfus Collection (Molinier, No. 13)
seems to prove. Also a plaquette at Dijon, reproduced in Art
Studies, 1930, fig. 19. The horse at the right throwing his head
sharply sideways is exactly repeated in Leone Leoni's Andrea
Doria Plaquette (Victoria and Albert Museum, No. A484-1910);
but a very similar sea-horse is already in an engraving by Mantegna, "The Combat of Tritons" (B.17), datable c. 1494, and this
composition might have inspired Leonardo.

At the top left of the drawing is a note in Leonardo's handwriting:
a bassa i chavalli (to lower the horses). This was tried out by
Leonardo in the Windsor drawing, 12591, of which a part is
reproduced in fig. 62. This drawing was always taken as a sketch
from Michelangelo's David ; but compare note 68 in Vasari's
"Life of Michelangelo", page 16 of this book. In fact, Leonardo
drew similar figures throughout his life, probably inspired by
antique sculptures ; a drawing in the British Museum (fig. 63),
datable about 1513, reminds one very much of Hellenistic statues,
like the bronze figure of a Hellenistic Ruler in the Terme Museum
at Rome (No. 544), or the numerous representations of Bacchus.

No. 58. ALLEGORY OF FORTUNA, BRITISH MUSEUM,
1895-9-15-482

This is, I think, Leonardo's most beautiful allegorical drawing,
but I do not understand at all what is meant by it. On the stump
of a tree lies a shield, and against the trunk leans a coat-of-arms
with a jumping lion. (For a similar escutcheon with lion and
dragon, symbolizing strength and prudence, see Richter § 692.)
But what do the curves under the shield represent ? They are
hardly fluttering ribbons, though they might be a flag, or even
the skin of a dragon. Above the shield, touching it with just the
toes of one foot, hovers a winged figure, probably meaning Fama.
This figure is beautifully shaded in a rather baroque way, and the
movement is strongly expressed by the streaming waves of
hair and drapery(1). There is another figure, running towards the
tree, holding her garment with one hand and touching the shield
with the other hand. The same figure, the head turned differently
and the hair more elaborately drawn, is repeated in the upper left
hand corner.

Fig. 61. Leda and the Swan. Freely copied from a lost painting, or cartoon, by Leonardo. Rome, Contessa Galotti Spiridon

(1) *The drapery reminds one of the angel on the right of the Fortiguerri monument at Pistoja, executed in Verrocchio's workshop 1478-83.*

Fig. 64. Allegory of Fortuna ("Occasio"). Painting on a chimney piece, once in the Palazzo Ducale at Mantua, probably after a design by Mantegna.

If Leonardo passed through Mantua on his way to Milan, as I suspect, he might have seen a chimney piece painting of "Fortuna" in the Ducal Palace. (Fig. 64.) The similarity consists, however, only in the subject and in the arrangement of the two main figures.

The figure at the right in Leonardo's drawing is, according to Edgar Wind (Old Master Drawings, March 1939, No. 52, p. 49), an 18th century addition. I think that only some of the silver point lines have been gone over in ink by a later hand; but, as the drawing is not for the time being accessible, I cannot confirm the extent to which this figure has been retouched.

There are two notes by Leonardo which may be connected with the Allegory of Fortuna. One note in Manuscript H-3, written 1493-94: "Galeazzo (Maria Sforza) between fair wind (*tempo tranquillo*) and the flight of Fortuna." The other note in Manuscript I-2, written 1498-99: "Il Moro representing Good Fortune, with hair, and robes, and his hands in front, and Messer Qualtieri taking him by the robes with a respectful air from below, having come in from the front." Those two notes are much later than the drawing in the British Museum, and they were written, the first when Galeazzo, the second when Ludovico was near his end.

No. 59. MADONNA WITH FRUIT-PLATE, LOUVRE, 101

For the drawing of the Child, compare plate 65.

No. 60. MADONNA WITH THE STOOL, UFFIZI, I, 421

The Child is sitting on a high stool and nursing a cat. Other drawings for a "Madonna with the Cat" are in the British Museum (1860-6-16-98; 1857-1-10-1), in the Musée Bonnat at Bayonne (No. 152), etc. Compare also No. 62.

No. 61. MADONNA WITH THE UNICORN, BRITISH MUSEUM, 1860-6-16-98

The whole sheet is 27.3 x 18.8 cm, but we have not reproduced the blank part of the paper. On the reverse are sketches for a Madonna with the Cat. Another drawing of the Virgin with the Unicorn is at the Ashmolean Museum in Oxford (Colvin I, 15A).

No. 62. STUDIES FOR A VIRGIN WITH THE CAT, BRITISH MUSEUM, 1856-6-21-1

Obverse and reverse of a sheet. No. 62A is traced through from 62, with various alterations; the head of the Virgin is sketched in three positions. A similar drawing is in the Collection of Arthur Hungersford Pollen, London (Vasari Society, Second series, part III, 1922, No. 5). Compare also note on No. 60.

No. 63. KNEELING MADONNA, ETC. WINDSOR, 12276r.

This is the *recto* of a sheet, the *verso* of which we reproduced as No. 8. The head of the Virgin is sketched in two positions.

No. 64. STUDIES FOR A MADONNA WITH THE FLOWER, BRITISH MUSEUM, 1860-6-16-100

Obverse and reverse of a sheet, which is 19.6 x 14.8 cm, but of which the blank part is not reproduced. The arch around the sketch (at the right of No. 64) shows that Leonardo considered a painting with an ogive top; compare No. 65 and No. 62.

The drawing 64A is a rather tentative one: the right arm and the head of the Virgin are sketched in two positions, and the lines in silverpoint are throughout very different from the pen-strokes.

No. 65. MADONNA BENOIS, HERMITAGE, LENINGRAD

Since 1914 in the Hermitage, formerly in the Collection of the painter Léon Benois (after whom the picture is named). One of Leonardo's earliest paintings, and one which was endlessly repeated, not only by Italian painters but also by the Flemish school. The best of these replicas is in the Galleria Colonna at Rome, ascribed to Filippino Lippi (Photo Alinari 7342). The Madonna alone was copied by Raphael, in his "Virgin with the Carnation" (of which the original is lost, but several copies thereof are known; cf. Crowe and Cavalcaselle, I, p. 273). The Child alone was very often copied, as, for instance, by Lorenzo di Credi in a Madonna painting in the Turin Gallery, No. 115 (Photo Alinari 14814).

The numerous repetitions of this little painting alone prove that it cannot have been by a second-rate painter.

The picture is not too well preserved; it suffered when it was transferred from panel to canvas; there are retouchings in the drapery, mouth, neck and hands of the Madonna, left knee and right hand of the child, most of the background, etc.

No. 66. THE ANNUNCIATION, UFFIZI, 1618 (1288)

Maud Cruttwell ascribed the picture to Verrocchio. Morelli considered it to be the work of Ridolfo Ghirlandajo, Berenson thought it a joint work of Credi and Leonardo. Baron Liphart, who was the first to claim the Benois Madonna for Leonardo, was also the first to claim this painting for the same Master; and he obviously proved to be right, as since the Leonardo Exhibition of 1939 most critics are agreed as to Leonardo's authorship of these two paintings. Many years ago I met Bode in front of the Uffizi Annunciation. He explained—in a most sarcastic way—that no one but Leonardo could be the painter of this panel, and he pointed out the close observation of nature in the drawing of the flowers and the foreground, and added that the painter must have studied a bird's wing in order to delineate the wings of the angel in such an "organic" way. He had no difficulty in persuading me.

Miss Cruttwell had already detected that the curious ornamentation of the reading-desk bore the strongest resemblance to Verrocchio's Medici Sarcophagus (fig. 65). I found a small drawing (fig. 66) in the Codex Atlanticus, which seemed to me still nearer in ornamental detail, though designed for a quite different purpose.

Fig. 65. Detail of the Medici Tomb by Verrocchio. 1472. Florence, San Lorenzo.   Fig. 66. Design for a bag, pen and ink drawing by Leonardo, in the Codice Atlantico. Milan, Ambrosiana.

Compare the ornamental detail of the reading-desk in plate No. 66.

In 1907 Sidney Colvin published the drawing for the right arm of the angel, which drawing is certainly by the young Leonardo (fig. 67).

THE ANNUNCIATION. C. 1474. FLORENCE, UFFIZI. (CF. PL. 66)

Fig. 67. Study for the right arm of the angel of the Annunciation (cf. plate 67).
Pen and ink drawing by Leonardo, c. 1472-74. Christ Church Library, Oxford.

The painting was originally in the Convent of Monte Oliveto near Florence, and was transferred to the Uffizi in 1867. It is rather badly preserved, obscured by dirty varnish, and much repainted, *e.g.* the lower part of the angel's draperies and most of the architecture.

No. 67.   THE ANGEL GABRIEL.   Detail of plate 66.

No. 68.   MADONNA WITH THE CARNATION, MUNICH, ÄLTERE PINAKOTHEK, 7779 (1493)

Cut at the left side, of about 1½ inches.

The picture is in a very poor condition, which can be seen even in the reproduction; the face of the Virgin, for instance, is nearly completely overpainted, forming a leathery *craquelure*. But, allowing for the bad preservation of the painting, a long list can be given connecting the Munich Madonna with the workshop of Verrocchio:

Fig. 68.   Drawing for the Head of a Madonna, by Verrocchio, c. 1475.   British Museum.

(1) Madonna by Credi, Munich 7820 (1016a).
(2) The Pistoja Altar-piece (Cruttwell, pl. 40).
(3) Madonna Dreyfus (Suida, pl. 5; in possession of Duveen).
(4) An altar-piece by Credi in Naples (Mackowsky, fig. 77).
(5) A silver-point drawing by Verrocchio (sometimes ascribed to Leonardo or Credi) in Dresden (Mackowsky, fig. 76).
(6) A Head of the Madonna in the Louvre, drawing (Suida, pl. 4: attributed to Leonardo).
(7) A Head by Verrocchio in the British Museum (fig. 68).

This list seems to call for some discussion, but as we lack space to give all the reproductions, the list itself might be useful to the student who wants comparative material. It is characteristic that most critics give to Leonardo a share in the Pistoja altar-piece, and that the drawing in Dresden and the drawing in London (fig. 68) are sometimes ascribed to Leonardo himself, on the basis of a passage in Vasari: "Heads of ladies of noble mien and with elaborately dressed hair [drawings by Verrocchio], which by reason of their beauty were imitated by Leonardo." Comparing now the black chalk drawing in the British Museum (fig. 68) with the Head of the Madonna in the Munich picture (plate 68), we certainly find the same eyes, mouth and hair-dress, and we can even assume that the same model was used. A comparison with the other paintings mentioned in the list (which could be extended) would give a similar result; the brooch and the long fold underneath are very significant.

The Munich picture was certainly executed in Verrocchio's workshop; the landscape, the draperies, and the drawing of the child all favour an attribution to Leonardo. But still it is an unpleasant picture.

No. 69.   STUDY FOR THE HEAD OF THE "MADONNA LITTA", LOUVRE, 2376

According to Berenson (Florentine Drawings, second edition, No. 1067C, and pag. 562), one of the earliest drawings by Leonardo. Demonts and Bodmer date it c. 1490-94.

No. 70.   MADONNA LITTA, HERMITAGE, LENINGRAD, No. 22 (Cat. 1891, No. 13a)

This picture is in a very bad condition, most of it being overpainted. The cloak of the Madonna which looks, but is not, unfinished, shows approximately the state of the painting without retouchings.

The picture is named after Conte Litta, Milan, in whose collection it was before it came to the Hermitage, in 1865.

Morelli attributed it to Bernardino de' Conti, but there is a replica by this painter in the Museo Poldi-Pezzoli in Milan (No. 639), which is very different from the Hermitage painting. Many other replicas of the Madonna Litta are known (*e.g.* in the Coll. of Conte Piero Ricci Oddi, Rome; Principe Borromeo, Milan; Howard Coll., New York). The composition was certainly famous as it was so often repeated. Compare also plate 69.

No. 71.   STUDY FOR THE ADORATION OF THE KINGS, LOUVRE, R.F.1978 (cf. pl. 72)

In March 1481 Leonardo made a contract with the monks of San Donato a Scopeto, a cloister outside Florence near the Porta Romana, to paint for them an altar-piece and to finish it in two years, or at most in two and a half years. The theme was "The Adoration of the Kings". The picture was never finished. (1)

A number of beautiful drawings are connected with this commission; we reproduce eight of them as Nos. 71, 76, 79, 124, 125, 126, 128, and 129. No. 71 represents Leonardo's first idea for the painting. The scene is the courtyard of a ruined palace; at the left are two arcades, at the right five arcades and two flights of stairs, leading to a gallery, on which a man is sitting and blowing a trumpet. In the background are many figures, among them men on horseback, somewhat similar to the later sketches for the Anghiari battle. Most of the figures are drawn in the nude, in order to delineate the movements in a manner anatomically correct. The arms of the man who gives the goblet to the child are sketched in two different positions. Ox and Ass appear again in No. 124. The drawing was formerly in the Gallichon Collection.

(1) *The commission was subsequently given to Filippino Lippi, who finished his "Adoration of the Kings" in March 1497 (1496, according to the Florentine calendar). The monastery of San Donato was destroyed during the siege of Florence in 1529; Filippino's "Adoration" is now in the Uffizi, No. 1566 (1257).*

Nos. 72-75. ADORATION OF THE KINGS, UFFIZI, 1594.

See the note on No. 71.

The picture is just "under-painted", a large drawing in umber brown over a sand-coloured priming. The most important figures—the Virgin and the Kings in the foreground—are the least finished ones. The picture was begun in March 1481; when Leonardo left for Milan (probably in the autumn of 1482) the painting remained with Amerigo Benci, the father of Ginevra (see plate 23). Professor Simon Meller expressed the opinion that Leonardo resumed his work during his later stay in Florence, *i.e.* 1503, when he was working on the cartoon of the Anghiari battle; Strzygowski accepted this view, and thought that some of the horses were added later. Although the whole picture looks as if it were done at one stroke, some of the drawings would seem to confirm this theory. The Head of a Horse, plate 126, was obviously used in the "Adoration" (cf. plate 127), and must therefore be dated c. 1481; if Meller's assumption is right, we should date the drawing according to its style, c. 1503. This theory, of course, rests on slender foundations,(1) but I mention it as being perhaps worthy of re-consideration.(2)

To understand how it was that Leonardo worked for so considerable a time at his "Adoration of the Kings" and still left it "unfinished", we may compare any one of Rembrandt's etchings, which, though of a different period and style, are nearest in artistic aim to Leonardo's "Adoration". Let us take one of the best known, the "Three Crosses" (B. 78). Here, as in Leonardo's "Adoration", stand some of the most important figures as white patches against the dark background or a dark group of figures. There exist many "states" of this etching, comprising a greater or lesser number of figures and different shadings; here we can follow all the stages of work at which in Leonardo's painting we can only guess. Although Rembrandt must have worked for a very long time at this etching, it does not show the least degree of "finish", not even as much as an average draughtsman could achieve in a few hours of work. We would not, however, call Rembrandt's Three Crosses unfinished; we can see quite well how the etching remained through all its states; and after all the laborious work done, the first creative idea was still in evidence like a brilliant improvisation. Leonardo's painting is no less finished than Rembrandt's etching.

This suggestion of "sketchiness", indication instead of definition, last thoughts which look like first thoughts, is not altogether a modern idea. Vasari refers to it, in the Life of Luca della Robbia, whose highly finished "Cantoria" he compares with that of Donatello which is, as he thinks, but a sketch. "Experience shows," says Vasari, "that all works of art seen at a distance, whether paintings or sculptures, are bolder and more vigorous to the eye, if merely done in the rough, than if laboriously finished. . . It often happens that these rapid sketches, which are thrown off suddenly in the first ardour of inspiration, express the idea perfectly in a few strokes; while too much care and labour, on the contrary, will often deprive the works of all force and character when the artist never knows when to take his hands off . . . The artist who visualizes from the first what he is going to create, invariably proceeds on his way towards perfect realization with ease. . . . Nevertheless, there are some, though they are rare, who can only do well when they proceed slowly . . as [among the poets] Bembo who expends months and even years in the production of a sonnet."

Leonardo was a slow worker, and he never brought the Sforza monument beyond the stage of a sketch, nor some of his finest pictorial compositions beyond the stage of a "cartoon". If we are to credit Vasari, he left the "Last Supper" and the Mona Lisa "unfinished", while we can see for ourselves that the Ambrosiana Musician, the Lady with the Ermine, and the Adoration of the Kings are all unfinished. But it is a moot point whether some works are capable of further elaboration without loss.

Leonardo's "Adoration of the Kings" has a charm which no reproduction can communicate, as all the modulation of the warm brown is lost in this process.

I have always thought that the drawing of the Virgin and the Child in this painting was inspired by a composition of Luca della Robbia (fig. 69), which in a similar way was also used for

(1) *It was refuted by Bode and Bodmer.*

(2) *In the Venice Academy there is a drawing by Cesare da Sesto, "The Adoration of the Kings", in which the Madonna closely resembles Raphael's Madonna of Foligno, which is rather Leonardesque, but the horses in the background are obviously taken from the "Battle of Anghiari" (Reprod. Morelli, Italian Painters, II, pag. 91).*

Fig. 69. Luca della Robbia: Madonna of the Roses. Enamelled terra-cotta relief, c. 1465. Florence, Bargello. (Compare plate 74.) 6604

a panel of Luca della Robbia's bronze door of Florence Cathedral, Sacristy. (The last panels of this door were cast in Verrocchio's workshop, 1467.)

No. 76. STUDY FOR THE BACKGROUND OF THE ADORATION OF THE KINGS, UFFIZI, I, 436.

See the notes on Nos. 71 and 72.

No. 77. STUDIES FOR THE ADORATION OF THE SHEPHERDS, FOR THE LAST SUPPER AND SKETCH OF A HYGROMETER, LOUVRE, 2258r.

On the back of this sheet is the drawing which is reproduced here as plate 80.

About three years before "The Adoration of the Kings", Leonardo contemplated an "Adoration of the Shepherds", and made a number of sketches, now reproduced as Nos. 77, 78, 80 and perhaps also No. 124, which might be related to the earlier version. This sheet is very interesting as it contains the earliest germ of the Last Supper.

The sketch of the hygrometer is accompanied by the note: "Mode of weighing the air and of knowing when the weather will change." A similar experiment was earlier made by Leon Battista Alberti in 1437, who fixed a dry sponge to the end of the arm of a balance, in order to weigh the moisture in the air which was absorbed by the sponge. (Alberti, Architettura, Venice, 1565, p. 366.) A more developed sketch for a hygrometer by Leonardo is in the Codice Atlantico, 249 verso, a.

No. 78. STUDY FOR THE ADORATION OF THE SHEPHERDS, MUSÉE BONNAT, 658

See note on No. 77. The paper is covered with a red preparation.

No. 79. STUDY FOR THE ADORATION OF THE KINGS, ECOLE DES BEAUX-ARTS, PARIS, 34555 A.

Some of the figures were actually used in the "Adoration of the Kings" (plate 72). The man with his hand on his chin (left side and centre below) is the first sketch for the philosopher (left end of the picture; cf. also plate 73); the figure group of four women appears in the painting at the foot of the stairs; the man shading his eyes and looking upwards is used in a different way; the woman (lower right) with her left arm bent and the head turned to the right is a sketch for the angel behind the tree.

No. 80. STUDY FOR THE ADORATION OF THE
SHEPHERDS, LOUVRE, 2258 verso.
See note on No. 77.

No. 81. STUDIES FOR THE ADORATION OF THE CHILD,
METROPOLITAN MUSEUM, NEW YORK.
The whole sheet is 16.2 x 19.5 cm, but we are not reproducing
the part which is blank.
Here an idea is developed which first appeared in the sketches
for "The Adoration of the Shepherds", cf. No. 78. This and the
following drawing are still closer to the "Adoration" than to the
"Madonna of the Rocks" (plate 83).
A passage in the Vasari biography refers to a *natività* painting
by Leonardo : "Ludovico Sforza begged Leonardo to paint an
altar-piece of the Nativity, which was sent by the Duke to the
Emperor."(1) As this painting is lost we cannot with any certainty
connect the drawings with it. Compare also plates 37 and 82.

No. 82. STUDY FOR THE ADORATION OF THE CHILD,
VENICE, 256.
The figure of St Joseph resembles a similar figure in a drawing
at Hamburg (No. 21488), which is on paper of the same kind
and which belongs to the same period as the drawing in the Musée
Bonnat, plate 78. This drawing is apparently a fragment of a
larger sheet, of which another fragment is preserved in the same
collection (No. 259), representing a kneeling shepherd, a flying
angel, and four nude children. The motive of the kneeling
Madonna was not new in Florence ; she appears (in this position)
in Hugo van der Goes' Portinari Altar-piece (c. 1476), and in three
early paintings by Filippo Lippi (c. 1455). The figure of a
kneeling mother with outstretched arms, on the bronze relief of
Ghiberti's Reliquari of St Zenobius in Florence Cathedral (finished
1442) may have inspired Leonardo's drawing, plate 81.

No. 83. MADONNA OF THE ROCKS, LOUVRE, No. 1599.
On 25th April 1483 Leonardo and the brothers Evangelista and
Ambrogio da Predis received the commission for this altar-piece
from the Confraternity of the Immaculate Conception, Milan. The
picture was probably finished in 1490, but a lawsuit followed, as
Ambrogio da Predis asked for a supplementary payment. Of the
work of Predis only an Angel survives in the National Gallery
(No. 1662), one of the two ordered as wings to the painting.
Adolfo Venturi suggested that King Louis XII took the painting
to France, which is credible enough, as that King even attempted to
carry away · Leonardo's Last Supper—"he employed architects to
frame it in wood and iron, so that it might be transported in safety,
without any regard for the cost, so great was his desire ; but the
King was thwarted by its being done on the wall, and it remained
in Milan," as we learn from Vasari. If Venturi is right, the
"Madonna of the Rocks" had already been in France for some
time when Leonardo came there ; we cannot, however, be certain
about this, as no mention is made of the picture being in France
until 1625, when it was at the Château de Fontainebleau.
In April, 1506, the Confraternity of the Conception agreed to
an additional payment, and soon afterwards the "Madonna of the
Rocks" was placed in their chapel, in the Church of San Francesco,
at Milan, where it remained until 1781. This painting, however,
was not the first version (now in the Louvre, plate 83), but a later
one (now in the National Gallery, London, plate 84). Whether
the first version was in the same chapel between 1490 and 1506,
and afterwards replaced by the second version—we do not know.
We can only say that the National Gallery picture came from the
Chapel of the "Confraternità della Concezione della Beata Vergine
Maria" in Milan, and that the Louvre picture was in the Collection
of the King of France at an early date.
The Louvre painting suffered when it was transferred from
panel to canvas (which was done c. 1800) ; it has been retouched
in many places, especially in the drapery of the Virgin, the lower
part of the background, etc.

---

(1) *According to Vasari, this painting, now lost, was done soon after
Leonardo's arrival in Milan. The Anonimo Gaddiano (ed. Frey,
p. 112) mentions the picture as being in the possession of Maximilian I,
and Carducho (Dialogos, p. 20) as in the Collection of Charles V.*

Fig. 70. The Virgin of the Grotto, engraving after a drawing by Mantegna for the central
panel of his triptych in the Uffizi, c. 1464.
*Compare the cave in Leonardo's Madonna of the Rocks, pl. 83. Similar grottoes,
were used in stage settings, and probably also in mystery plays.*

Nos. 84-86. MADONNA OF THE ROCKS, NATIONAL
GALLERY, LONDON, 1093

See note on No. 83. Since 1785 in England, since 1880 in the
National Gallery. A later version of the Louvre picture (pl. 83),
re-designed by Leonardo. He probably began the painting and
put in occasional touches.

No. 87. VIRGIN AND CHILD WITH ST ANNE AND
THE INFANT ST JOHN, LOUVRE, No. 1598

There are at least three versions of Leonardo's St Anne
composition.
(a) The first Milanese version, done shortly before Leonardo left
the town, c. 1499 (Cartoon in the Royal Academy, London).
See plate 88.
(b) The Florentine version, as described by Fra Pietro da Novellara,
1501. (See Documents, No. XI.) This cartoon is lost.
(c) The second Milanese version, done during Leonardo's sub-
sequent stay in the town, 1506-11. Painting in the Louvre;
cartoon lost. (See plate 87.)
There are, besides, a number of tentative drawings, which, in
my opinion, do not correspond with either of the three versions
but suggest independent solutions. (See plates 89 and 89A.)
Most of the Louvre painting was done by pupils ; only the
landscape, the figure of St Anne and the right arm of the Virgin
are outstanding. It might be thought that the assistant was Melzi,
but in this case it is inexplicable why Melzi did not finish the
picture, inasmuch as he took it with him to Italy, after Leonardo's
death.
In 1517, Cardinal Luigi d'Aragona saw the "St Anne" in Leonardo's studio (cf. Documents, No. XVI). We know how the
picture returned to Italy, but we do not know how it came just to
Casale, a town on the river Po. In 1630, when Cardinal Richelieu
crossed into Italy to settle the Mantuan succession question by

war, he found Leonardo's "St Anne" in Casale and brought it back with him to Paris; six years later he gave it to the King of France, and since 1801 it has been in the Louvre.

Compare plates 34, 38, 39. (1)

No. 88. CARTOON FOR THE VIRGIN AND CHILD WITH ST ANNE AND THE INFANT ST JOHN, ROYAL ACADEMY, LONDON, 183

See note on No. 87.

The cartoon(2) was in Milan until 1721; then in Venice, where it was bought by Robert Udny, the brother of the English Ambassador, in 1763. It became the property of the Royal Academy at a date prior to the 23rd March 1791.

No. 89. STUDY FOR THE VIRGIN AND ST ANNE, ACADEMY, VENICE, 230

See note on No. 87.

The head of St Anne is sketched in two different positions.

No. 89A. STUDY FOR THE VIRGIN AND ST ANNE, LOUVRE, R.F. 460.

See note on No. 87.

The child is nursing a lamb, but only a close study of the drawing will discover the meaning of the lines.

No. 90. SKETCH FOR THE LAST SUPPER, VENICE, 254

This is a very important drawing as far as the composition is concerned. In my opinion, it is a copy, by a pupil, after Leonardo's first cartoon for the Last Supper; the names of the Apostles are added in Leonardo's handwriting. No. 90A shows how the cartoon must have looked originally: the sheet used for the Venice Academy drawing was too short to take all the figures, the four Apostles who should be at the left are placed underneath, but the shoulder and arm of one of them are given twice, with all the accidental features of the sketch exactly repeated. Otherwise the copy is rather weak, the hands especially being awkwardly drawn; but the copyist followed the original very closely as he even imitated the shading from left to right. (Cf. Beltrami, in *Boll. della Racc. Vinc.* 1910.)

In this first sketch Leonardo followed the Florentine tradition in placing Judas isolated on one side of the table and figuring St John sleeping with his head on his arms; we find the same arrangement of figures in Castagno's "Cenacolo" at Florence (fig. 71); but Francesco Botticini's representation of the same theme on a small panel in Empoli bears still more similarity with Leonardo's Last Supper (fig. 72).

---

(1) *I think it is better to puzzle the student than to make things appear plainer than they really are. What is stated above is what I believe, but I note that the critics are not agreed on all these points, especially as regards the dating. Professor Hildebrandt dates the London cartoon (a) from the beginning of the Milanese period, i.e. 1483-94; Bodmer after 1500, i.e. from the second Florentine period; Seidlitz was of the same opinion as Hildebrandt; Popp and Clark dated it towards the end of the Milanese period, i.e. about 1498. About the dating of the second cartoon (b) there is no difference of opinion, as it is documented by Novellara's letter of 1501. The sole question is whether this cartoon was taken by Leonardo to France or not. It was certainly not used for the Louvre picture, as the figures in this second cartoon were turned to the left, and as seems to be proved by a free version by Andrea Bresciano, Berlin Museum, No. 230; a similar picture in the Prado, No. 349; by Raphael's "Holy Family with the Lamb" of 1507, in the same Museum, No. 296; and by Luini's "Madonna with the two Children" of 1530, in Lugano, in which painting the Infant Christ nursing the Lamb is exactly the same as in Bresciano's picture. About the third version (c) opinions are again divided. Gabriel Rouchès doubted whether the (lost) cartoon and the Louvre painting were executed in Italy before 1515, or in France, c. 1516-17. On the other hand, such an expert as Popp thought (p. 45) that the composition was finished before 1504. My dating of 1506-10 is in accordance with Seidlitz, Bodmer and Clark.*

(2) *This cartoon is not identical with the one described by Fra Pietro Novellara in 1501 (see Documents, No. XI) which was done for an altar-piece in S. Annunciata after Filippino Lippi had resigned the commission in favour of Leonardo. The altar-piece was never executed by Leonardo and the cartoon is lost. Padre Sebastiano Resta (c. 1680), who saw the other cartoon (plate 88) in Milan, in the Collection of Conte Arconati, stated that it was done for King Louis XII, which would be after the fall of Milan, in the autumn of 1499.*

Fig. 71.   Andrea del Castagno: Last Supper, fresco (part), c. 1450. Florence, Apollonia.

Fig. 72.   Francesco Botticini: Last Supper, Predella-panel, 1484-91.   Empoli, Galleria della Collegiata.

Botticini finished his work about five years before Leonardo; he was for some time connected with the Verrocchio workshop, and Leonardo passed repeatedly through Empoli, which is a small town between Florence and Pisa, near the the place where Leonardo was born.

No. 91. CHRIST CARRYING HIS CROSS, VENICE, 231

This small drawing shows just the head of Christ crowned with thorns, and the hand of a beadle clutching the hair. It seems feasible that of this composition Leonardo executed not only one but two cartoons, which are lost and now known only by different imitations.

In the first cartoon Christ was turned to the left (as in the drawing), and I imagine that Leonardo took this cartoon with him to Venice, as all imitations I know of this version belong to the Venetian School.(3) I reproduce here two variants; the one, in a very poor state of preservation, is usually ascribed to Giorgione (fig. 73); the other painting originated in the workshop of Giovanni Bellini, and at least three copies are extant; the best of the three, though the least Bellinesque, is thought to be a copy by Giorgione, or by Palma Vecchio (fig. 74).

In the other, and later, version Christ was turned to the right, and this composition was imitated only by Milanese painters. The most beautiful of these adaptations is Sodoma's fresco in Monte Oliveto Maggiore (fig. 76); Solario's painting is rather similar in drawing but much less Leonardo-like in spirit.(4)

No. 92. HEAD OF CHRIST, BRERA, 280

This drawing is in the worst state possible, half destroyed and overpainted with pastels, but it still retains its magic. I think it gives a much better idea of how the head of Christ in The Last Supper looked originally than what is left of it in the wall-painting itself (plate 94). It has been doubted, of course, many times, *e.g.* by G. Carotti, who ascribed it to Cesare da Sesto; and it has been zealously defended, *e.g.* by Prof. Hildebrandt (in his Leonardo book, 1927, pp. 98-101). It is the ghost of a Leonardo drawing; worse still, it is a rouged and made-up ghost; but it remains the only visible thing we can take hold of if we want to dream how Leonardo painted the central figure of his masterpiece.

There are two notes by Leonardo which prove that he made studies from living persons, meaning to use their features as a

---

(3) *Leonardo was in Venice in the spring of 1500, the only sojourn of which we have documentary evidence, but no doubt he was there before and after that date, and most probably in 1506, as his influence on the art of Bellini and Giorgione is most apparent about this time. Apart from the copies reproduced as figures 73 and 74, there are many other variants of less value, e.g. one in Dresden (No. 222, attributed to Romanino) and a manneristic painting in the former Crespi Collection (Photo Anderson, No. 3485).*

(4) *I cannot give a list of the other copies, as they are too numerous; one of them, by Luini, in the Poldo Pezzoli Museum at Milan, is well known; others are at Vienna and Rome.*

Figs. 73-76. Christ bearing his Cross. 73 : attributed to Giorgione (or Titian), 1500-1506. Venice, San Rocco.—74 : attributed to Giorgione (copy after Giovanni Bellini), 1500-1506.
Boston, Isabella Stewart Gardner Museum.—75 : by Andrea Solario, 1511. Rome, Galleria Borghese.—76 : by Sodoma, 1506-08, Monte Oliveto Maggiore.

model for the figure of Christ in the Last Supper. One of the
notes reads, "Christ. Count Giovanni, the one with the Cardinal
of Mortaro" (S.K. II-1, 3a). The other, "Allesandro Carissimo
of Parma, for the hand of Christ" (same note-book, 9a).

No. 93. THE LAST SUPPER, SANTA MARIA DELLE GRAZIE, MILAN

See Documents, Nos. VII and VIII.

Painted at the instance of Duke Ludovico Moro for the dining-
room of the Cloister of the Dominican monks of Santa Maria
delle Grazie. The building is no longer used as a convent, but
Leonardo's painting is still there, or at least the ruins of it, as our
reproduction shows. A door was cut through the middle of the
lower part of the painting. Already Leonardo's contemporaries
were complaining about the poor state of preservation of the Last
Supper. What we can see of it at the present time is the original
grand composition which could not be obliterated, patches of the

old paint here and there, and the work of generations of restorers.
The first restoration took place in 1726, the next in 1770 ; during
the French occupation, 1796-1815, the painting was exposed to
much damage ; in 1800 the Refectory was used as a forage-room
by the soldiers ; afterwards, between 1820 and 1908, it was
thoroughly restored three times. And yet this greatest of paintings,
prior to Michelangelo's Sistine Chapel Frescoes, still radiates
vitality, just as a tragedy of Sophocles speaks to us again even in
the poorest translation, or the Elgin Marbles through mutilated
and broken fragments.

Thousands of pages have been written about this single painting;
the best of these books are mentioned in my bibliography ; I
cannot hope to add to their conclusions in these few paragraphs.

Some beautiful drawings were left finished by Leonardo in
preparation for his wall-painting—see Nos. 17, 18, 19 ; 90, 92 ;
and fig. 11.

No. 94. CHRIST. Detail of pl. 93.

No. 95. THE APOSTLES ST BARTHOLOMEW, ST JAMES THE LESS AND ST ANDREW.   Detail of pl. 93

No. 96. THE APOSTLES ST THOMAS, ST JAMES THE GREAT AND ST PHILIP.   Detail of pl. 93

Nos. 97-98 ST JEROME, PINACOTECA VATICANA, 151. Panel, unfinished.

The authenticity of this painting has never been doubted, though there is no literary documentation to it and it is not mentioned in any of the old Leonardo biographies. Poggi and Rinaldis assume that it was painted immediately before Leonardo left for Milan (1) i.e., about 1481-82. (Cf. the head in the middle of plate 75, which is of the same period.)

The painting was found by Cardinal Fesch (c. 1820) in a second-hand wardrobe, in Rome; it was being used as the door of a small wardrobe, the head of the Saint being cut out. The Cardinal, an uncle of Napoleon, was lucky enough to find the missing part of the panel a few years later—in the workshop of a cobbler, who was using the board as a table-top. In 1845, six years after the Cardinal's death, Pius IX bought the restored painting for his Gallery.

No. 99. ST JOHN THE BAPTIST, WINDSOR, 12572

According to Valentiner, a sketch for a figure in the Pistoja altar-piece. See our note on fig. 32, page 21; also note 66, page 15. In 1478 Leonardo was in Pistoja; this drawing is probably of the same time.

No. 100. ST JOHN THE BAPTIST, LOUVRE, No. 1597

See Document XVI, page 20; also fig. 8, page 8.

Louis XIII of France gave the picture to Charles I, in exchange for a painting by Holbein and one by Titian. In 1649, when the King's collection was sold by auction, Leonardo's St John was bought by the banker Jabach on behalf of Cardinal Mazarin, from whom the picture passed to Louis XIV.

No. 101. COURTYARD OF A FOUNDRY, WINDSOR, 12647

The drawing shows groups of naked men raising the barrel of a large gun, by means of a crane and levers. Compare Document I, item 7, on page 17.

No. 102. A COPSE OF BIRCHES, WINDSOR, 12431 recto

The whole sheet is 19.1 x 15.3 cm. The blank part is not reproduced. The verso of the drawing contains the sketch of a single tree, and a note of how light and shade have to be treated in the drawing of trees (Richter § 456).

No. 103. RIVER LANDSCAPE, WINDSOR, 12398

No. 104. A BIRD'S-EYE VIEW OF A RIVER LANDSCAPE, WITH A FERRY BOAT, WINDSOR, 12400

This drawing and No. 103 are probably of the same date as the Codex "About the Flight of Birds", 1505, at the Royal Library, Turin. Similar sketches, e.g., in Manuscript K, are slightly earlier.

No. 105. ARNO LANDSCAPE, DATED 1473, UFFIZI, Cat. V, 8 P

The inscription reads, in translation: "The day of the Holy Virgin of the Snows, August the 2nd, 1473". This is Leonardo's earliest dated drawing, done when he was 21 and still in Verrocchio's workshop. Seidlitz thought the drawing represents a landscape near Leonardo's birthplace, on the way from Vinci to Pistoja. The verso contains a sketch in black chalk, gone over with pen, of a mountainous landscape, with a bridge, the pen-and-ink sketch of a naked running man, and a head; also the note, "Io morando danto sono contento".

No. 106. THE DELUGE, WINDSOR, 12376 (cf. No. 110)

Earlier than the other drawings of the "Deluge series", Windsor Nos. 12377-86, of which two are reproduced as plates 111 and 112.

_____

(1) Was this picture done in competition with Perugino? Vasari states that Perugino, while he studied in Florence under Verrocchio, painted a "St Jerome in Penitence" on a wall in the cloister of Camaldoli, and that this mural was "much valued by the Florentines and greatly praised because he had made the saint old, lean and shrivelled, and wasted to a skeleton".

This drawing shows: horsemen thrown to the ground by a hurricane, and an uprooted tree in the lower right corner—this part of the drawing is also reproduced in actual size as No. 110. In the distance are seen the whirling waves of the sea, clouds, and Storm Gods blowing through pipes or trumpets. The group of six Wind Gods at the left recalls the trumpet-blowing angels in Michelangelo's "Last Judgement". (2)

No. 107. RAVINE WITH WATER-BIRDS, WINDSOR, 12395

Compare No. 105; but this drawing is probably later, as it shows a certain resemblance to the landscape in the St Jerome painting, plate 97.

No. 108. STORM IN THE ALPS, WINDSOR, 12409

Popp and Clark dated it c. 1499-1500. I imagine that these bird's-eye view landscapes were drawn at the time when Leonardo was most interested in the problems of aviation. There is a note in the Leicester Manuscript (Richter § 1060), datable c. 1504-1505, about the weather in the Alps, which reads like a text to this illustration.

(Compare also Richter § 1428A, datable 1505.)

No. 109. STORM IN A BAY, WINDSOR, 12401

See No. 106; and Nos. 111-112.

No. 110. DETAIL OF No. 106

Nos. 111 and 112. THE DELUGE, WINDSOR, 12379, 12377

Two of the ten drawings at Windsor Castle, which form a series; certainly of a late period, when Leonardo studied intensively the movement of water. Popp ascribed this series even to Leonardo's last years, after 1516. A comparison of figs. 77 and 77A shows that Leonardo used "swirling lines" to represent the movements of water and air, as was conventionally done in oriental art.

Figs. 77-77a. Waves, in Western and Eastern Art.—(77) Detail of a drawing by Leonardo, Windsor, No. 12384.—(77a) Woodcut from Hokusai's "Mangwa", vol. VII.

No. 113. STUDIES OF FLOWERS, VENICE, ACADEMY

Shaded from left to right, but unusually hard outlines, and therefore doubtful. Walter Pater praised the drawing as one of Leonardo's most beautiful. A similar, but much weaker drawing, once at Windsor Castle, was tentatively ascribed to Melzi and connected with his "Columbine" at the Hermitage. Amoretti (1804, p. 171) mentions a Flora painting, "disegnata da Lionardo, e dipinta da Francesco Melzi"—perhaps this study of flowers was done for the "Flora".

No. 114. FLOWERING RUSHES, WINDSOR, 12430 recto

On the verso a study of a bulrush. Sir Kenneth Clark thinks that "this was done in connection with the kneeling Leda"— see plate 56. Similar rushes also in the pen-and-ink sketch of a kneeling angel in the British Museum (1913-6-17-1; Vas. Soc. IX, 1).

_____

(2) Michelangelo's Paintings, Phaidon Edition, plate 158.

No. 115. LILY, WINDSOR, 12418

The earliest of Leonardo's botanical studies, done in a style different from the later drawings; the technique resembles most the character of the early drapery studies. I thought for some time it might have been a preparatory study for an altar-piece for San Franceso in Brescia; Leonardo received the commission for it in 1497, but never executed the painting. There is a note in Manuscript I-2, 107a (Richter § 679), "Anthony, a lily and a book". 1497, though, seems too late as a date for Leonardo's drawing, which is of the same period as the St John, plate 99. A similar stalk of a lily is in Gabriel's hand in the painting "Tobias and the Three Archangels", Florence, Uffizi (No. 8359; photo Alinari 1450), attributed to Francesco Botticini, or Verrocchio's workshop.

Nos. 116-119. STUDIES OF PLANTS, WINDSOR, 12420 recto, 12419, 12424, 12429

Sir Kenneth Clark connects all these botanical studies with Leonardo's two Leda cartoons (The kneeling and the standing Leda; plate 56 and fig. 61. See Clark, p. 57).

No. 120. STUDY OF A TREE, WINDSOR, 12417

I am following Berenson in the assumption that the drawing in black chalk was done by Leonardo and gone over in pen-and-ink by a pupil. Gustavo Frizzoni proved (1) that this pupil was Cesare da Sesto; only he went too far in giving the whole drawing to him. Frizzoni reproduced, as his proof, a sheet from Cesare da Sesto's sketch book in the Pierpont Morgan Library; but the tree in that Adam and Eve drawing seems to me incomparably weaker. I am of opinion that there is another drawing by Leonardo at Windsor (12339 recto), which was also re-drawn by Cesare da Sesto; it represents a part of the Anghiari battle cartoon (fig. 78). I think my theory explains why Sir Kenneth Clark was able to say, "the touch seems to be that of Leonardo, especially in the more rapidly drawn parts", while he described some features of the drawing as "typical of Cesare da Sesto", and the shading done by the right hand. This drawing, like the drawing of the tree, was claimed for Cesare da Sesto by Frizzoni and others. I think that both drawings contain much more of Leonardo's spirit than of his somewhat academic pupil's.

Fig. 78. Leonardo and Cesare da Sesto: Horsemen, sketch for a part of the Anghiari battle cartoon, black chalk drawing. Windsor.

No. 121. STUDIES OF CATS, WINDSOR, 12363

Companion sheet to plate 122. Sir Kenneth Clark is certainly right that "perhaps the majority of these studies have been inked in by a pupil".

No. 122. STUDIES OF ST GEORGE AND THE DRAGON, WINDSOR, 12331

Companion sheet to plate 121. Other studies for horsemen fighting a dragon are at the Louvre (bequest of Baron Edmond de Rothschild; reprod. Richter I, pl. XXXIIIA) and in the Ashmolean Museum, Oxford (reprod. by Colvin); a studio copy of a small drawing at the Ambrosiana, Milan (reprod. Rosenberg fig. 33; Photo Braun No. 75043). A note of 1492 by Leonardo, how to draw an imaginary animal (a dragon) so that it should appear natural, is transliterated in Richter § 585.

---

(1) Certain studies by Cesare da Sesto in relation to his pictures, by Gustavo Frizzoni, in Burlington Magazine, XXVI, 1914, pp. 187-194.

No. 123. BEETLE AND DRAGON-FLY, TURIN, ROYAL LIBRARY. Berenson, No. 1093

Two separate drawings, cut out and pasted on a small piece of paper.

No. 124. ASS AND OX, WINDSOR, 12362

Probably a sketch for animals in an Adoration of the Shepherds (compare plates 77, 78, 80).

No. 125. HEADS OF HORSES, WINDSOR, 12285

No. 126. HEAD OF A HORSE, WINDSOR, 12327 recto

No. 125 is one of the earliest drawings for the horses in the background of the Adoration (plate 72); No. 126 is one of the latest. See also Nos. 128 and 128A.

No. 126 was actually used in the painting—compare the detail photograph, reproduced as No. 127. This drawing is a fragment of the same sheet as the large drawing, reproduced as No. 129, but this does not prove that Nos. 126 and 129 are of the same period (2). No. 126 is done in line and wash, a technique which Leonardo mostly used between 1480 and 1485. (See Clark, p. 91; and plate 58.)

No. 127. DETAIL OF PLATE 72

No. 128. HORSEMAN. In the possession of Captain Norman R. Colville, from the collection of Henry Oppenheimer.

Study for the background of the Uffizi Adoration, but not used.

No. 128A. HORSEMAN. Collection of J. N. Brown, formerly Holford.

A study for the Horseman between the two trees in the background of the Adoration (plate 72). A very similar one of two horsemen is in a drawing in the possession of Charles Clarke, London (reprod. Bodmer, p. 148, and Burlington Magazine, 1925, XLVII, p. 275).

No. 129. STUDIES FOR THE BATTLE OF ANGHIARI, WINDSOR, 12336 recto (3)

See notes 46 and 47 to the "Life" by Vasari, page 12; also fig. 18 and 78; and plates 6, 7, 46, 47, 130-136.

No complete copy of the lost Anghiari cartoon is preserved—only a few original sketches (see our reproductions, as mentioned above), many more studies of horses, and a much retouched head of a warrior in Oxford. There are many copies of the centre scene, the Fight for the Standard, including one drawing in the Louvre, attributed to the school of Rubens (cf. fig. 18). Michelangelo and Raphael copied some other parts of Leonardo's cartoon (figs. 79 and 80). But I think Jacques Callot must have known the cartoon, or a good copy of it, as the red chalk drawings of battle scenes which he did at Florence in c. 1616, show a striking resemblance to scenes which we know from original Leonardo drawings and from copies of the "Battle for the Standard". (See fig. 81.)

Nos. 130-135. STUDIES FOR THE BATTLE OF ANGHIARI, WINDSOR, 12336 and 12340; VENICE, ACADEMY, 215 and 215A; BRITISH MUSEUM, 1854-5-13-17; VENICE, 216

See note on No. 129, also plates 47 and 46; and figs. 78-81.

---

(2) If a later date, i.e., 1503-1506, were acceptable for No. 126, it would strengthen Professor Meller's hypothesis that "the horses in the background of the Adoration were added during Leonardo's second Florentine period".

(3) The reverse of No. 129 contains a sketch of the solar system and notes on astronomy; also a sketch for the head of a horse in the Battle for the Standard (cf. fig. 18). This small sketch bears a superficial resemblance to the drawing which is reproduced here as pl. 126, but the ears are differently drawn and so is the mane. No. 126 and No. 129 are parts of the same sheet, though they are, as I believe, of different periods. No. 126 has a curious relationship to an antique bronze head of a horse which was once used as a fountain in the Medici Palace (now Florence, Museo Archeologico, No. 426, phot. Alinari 2537).

79   80   81

Figs. 79-81. Copies of parts of Leonardo's Anghiari battle cartoon. (79) Detail of a pen-and-ink drawing by Michelangelo, c. 1504. British Museum.—(80) Detail of a silver-point drawing by Raphael, c. 1506. Ashmolean Museum, Oxford.—(81) Detail of a red chalk drawing by Callot, c. 1616. Florence, Uffizi.

No. 136. STUDY FOR THE BATTLE OF ANGHIARI : CLOSE FIGHTING OF TWO SOLDIERS, VENICE, ACADEMY

Sketches by Michelangelo (Ashmolean Museum, Oxford ; Frey 157, Robinson 69), called "Samson slaying the Philistine" and done, according to Robinson, for a small relief, seem to be derived from Leonardo's drawing. (1) As Leonardo himself made so little use of the richness of his own ideas, it is most helpful to the understanding to watch their development by later artists—including Raphael, Michelangelo and Dürer.

No. 137. STUDY FOR THE TRIVULZIO MONUMENT, WINDSOR, 12356 recto

Leonardo made preparatory studies for two equestrian monuments : that of Francesco Sforza, from 1483 to 1496, and that of Marshal Giacomo Trivulzio (2) probably 1508-1512. The first monument certainly reached the model stage (see Documents, I, item 10 ; and II-VI). The reproductions, plates 137-147, give a quite good selection of Leonardo's different ideas for the two monuments with a pacing and with a prancing horse, but the various problems connected with it are too complicated to be dealt with here. (For an excellent survey, see Clark, Windsor Drawings, pp. XL-XLVI.)

(1) C. J. Holmes in his beautiful essay on Leonardo (in vol. IX of the Proceedings of the British Academy, 1919) emphasized how much Michelangelo was influenced by Leonardo. Discussing the "Adoration" (pl. 72) he remarks : "In fact the grand style which was to be perfected thirty years later on the Sistine ceiling is anticipated here, while among the studies for the picture are two from which Michelangelo did not disdain to borrow the idea of his famous 'Slaves' in the Louvre some forty years later." Michelangelo's design of 1513 for the Julius tomb contains the same fettered prisoners as Leonardo's sketch of the Trivulzio monument of c. 1511 (see No. 137). About Michelangelo's angels blowing the last trumpets, see note to No. 106.

(2) See Richter § 725 for a specified estimate by Leonardo for this monument from Codex Atlanticus, fol. 179-B.

The drawing, plate 137, shows a walking horse, whose one foreleg rests on a helmet ; horse and horseman are placed on a high monument which contains, in a cornice, the sarcophagus and a recumbent figure of the deceased lying on it. Leonardo intended to adorn the monument with "six harpies with candelabra". (3) The horse was to be life-size, so the complete monument—as given in this sketch—would have been about 21 feet high.

No. 138. STUDY FOR THE SFORZA MONUMENT, WINDSOR, 12358 recto

This and No. 143 belong to Leonardo's latest and finest silver-point drawings ; he did not use that technique after 1490.

The arms of the rider are tentatively sketched in different directions : the left arm, holding the reins, once near the mane, and once drawn back ; the right arm with the baton once stretched forward and once backward. The prostrate foe holds a shield over his head. "Leonardo has introduced the device of a prostrate foe, in imitation perhaps of Pollajuolo, perhaps of some classical relief" (Clark, p. 41). Of Pollajuolo's design two copies are extant, one at Munich (fig. 83) and one in the collection of Philip Hofer, New York. Pollajuolo's sketches for an equestrian monument must have been done in direct competition with Leonardo. (4)

(3) The figures lightly sketched at the corners of the monument indicate captives tied to columns.

(4) I am, however, inclined to believe L. Courajod (Léonard da Vinci et le statue de Francesco Sforza, Paris 1879, p. 50) and S. Meller (Prussian Jahrbuch XXXVII, 1916, p. 230) that the Munich drawing is not an independent design by Pollajuolo, but reproduces a small model by Leonardo ; this lost model was probably executed in wax. Sodoma, who was powerfully influenced by Leonardo from 1498 to 1500 in Milan, gave in a later painting (fig. 84) the prostrate foe in the same position as Pollajuolo. The same model is used in Bacchiaca's "Life of St Acasius" in the Uffizi, Florence (Frizzoni, in Arch. stor. dell' Arte, 1895, p. 3). It has been surmised that small models or drawings by Leonardo were copied in the rearing horse of Heliodorus in a Vatican mural by Raphael, and in a pacing horse in Dürer's engraving "Knight, Death and Devil" ; both, the engraving and the mural, were done in 1513.

82   83   84

Figs. 82-84. Horseman and prostrate foe.—(82) Medicean Gem. Etching in Leonardo Agostini's "Le Gemme Antiche Figurate", vol. II, 1669.—(83) Drawing after Antonio Pollajuolo's model for the Sforza monument, c. 1480-1490. Munich, Print room.—(84) Sodoma : Santiago riding over Sarazens, 1530. Fresco in the Spanish Chapel of San Spirito, Siena.

The *motif* of the galloping rider trampling down an enemy is known from Roman coins—*e.g.*, one of Lucius Verus, and from antique gems—*e.g.*, Furtwängler XXV, 52. But a cameo, once in the Medici Collection (fig. 82), shows the foe defending himself with his shield in a very similar position to that in some of Leonardo's drawings, especially when he reverted to the same idea for the Trivulzio monument (cf. plate 146). See also note to No. 147.

Nos. 139-141. SKETCHES IN PREPARATION FOR CAST-
ING THE BRONZE HORSE. Codex Atlanticus,
fol. 216 verso; Windsor, 12351 verso and 12349 recto

In November 1494 Ludovico Sforza sent all the bronze collected for the casting of the Monument to his brother-in-law, the Duke of Ferrara, who used it for the founding of guns.

Leonardo's handwriting on the three sketches reproduced here is transliterated in Richter §§ 712-714.

Horse and rider of the Sforza monument were to be of colossal proportions, according to Pacioli about 22 feet high.

No. 142. STUDIES FOR THE TRIVULZIO MONUMENT,
WINDSOR, 12344 recto

See notes to No. 137.

No. 143. STUDIES FOR THE SFORZA MONUMENT,
WINDSOR, 12321

See notes to Nos. 137 and 138.

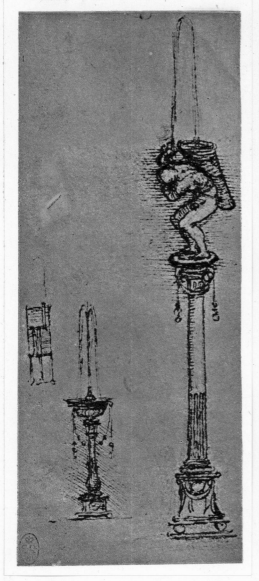

Fig. 86. Designs for a Fountain, pen-and-ink drawing, Windsor (12690).

Nos. 144, 145, 146. STUDIES FOR THE TRIVULZIO MONU-
MENT, WINDSOR, 12354, 12360, 12355.

See notes to Nos. 137 and 138.

The figure of the rider, lifting up his right arm, and the figure of the man under the hoofs of the horse recall Leonardo's sketch for the Anghiari battle, of the close fighting of two soldiers (plate 136).

The most interesting part of plate 146 are the designs of the elaborate base on which horse and rider were to be placed. Neither Donatello's Gattamelatta nor Verrocchio's Colleoni stand on such a triumphal arch; Baroncelli's equestrian monument of 1454 at Ferrara was the only possible model, as Leon Battista Alberti (1) had designed for it a base with arches. Unfortunately this monument was destroyed during the French Revolution.

The single sketch in plate 145, gone over with pen, shows a rather curious idea: the equestrian monument adapted as a fountain; the horse, pacing like a courser in a circus, is tilting a vase with his left fore-leg, and the water is pouring down into a basin, while the right hind-leg of the horse rests on a tortoise.

(1) *A. Venturi, in L'Arte XVII, 1914, pag. 153 et seq.*

Fig. 85. School of Leonardo: Engraving after small-scale models for the Sforza monument.
British Museum. (cf. pl. 147.)

*All we know for certain about Leonardo as a sculptor is founded on his
drawings for the two equestrian monuments (compare plates 137-146). The
following survey and the plates 147-150 give some information about the
sculptures attributed to him.*

Figs. 87-89. Three terracotta busts of St. John, wrongly attributed to Leonardo, but perhaps in imitation of some lost busts by him.
(87): Ex-Stroganoff Collection, Rome. (88): Ex-Hainauer Collection, Berlin.
(89): Victoria and Albert Museum.

Nos. 147-150. LEONARDO AS A SCULPTOR

The question of Leonardo's sculptural work teems with complicated problems, as no authenticated work is extant which could serve as basis for an analysis of style. What we can offer here is not a discussion but a survey and list of sculptures attributed to Leonardo.

I. LITERARY DOCUMENTATIONS

Vasari (1568) mentions "heads of smiling women and of children executed in gypsum". Lomazzo (1584) speaks of "*una testicciula di terra di propria mano di Leonardo da Vinci*", i.e., the terracotta head of an infant Christ, in his collection; and of "*un cavallo di rilievo di plastica, fatto di sua mano*", i.e., a relief—or full relief?—of a horse, in the collection of the sculptor Leone Leoni in Milan. Cardinal Federigo Borromeo (1625) saw an infant Christ made of gypsum by Leonardo, which was used as a model by Luini for one of his paintings. (1) Leonardo himself, in a note of c. 1482, mentions "a representation of the Passion made in relief". (2)

(1) *Amoretti*, 160.
(2) *Richter* § 680, item 33.

II. DRAWINGS BY LEONARDO CONNECTED WITH SCULPTURE

There are many drawings done as studies for the two equestrian monuments of Francesco Sforza and Marshal Trivulzio (pl. 137-146 are a small selection).

There is a drawing at Windsor (12328), with a note by Leonardo

Fig. 90. Detail of a drawing by Leonardo, with the inscription "fanne un picholo di cera lugho un dito", c. 1506. Windsor. (Cf. Clark, pag. 23.)

that he should not forget to make small models in wax of the horses and men drawn (fig. 90). This note can be connected with the horseman in Budapest (plate 147) and similar bronzes. The bust of the infant Christ, mentioned by Vasari, Lomazzo and Cardinal Borromeo, appears in sketches at Windsor (12519 and 12567), one of which is reproduced here (fig. 91). A drawing at Windsor (12357) and an engraving at the British Museum (fig. 85) contain traces of small-scale models for the Sforza monument. Other drawings give ideas for fountains (Windsor 12690, 12691; fig. 86. See also the "David" and the horseman as fountains, fig. 63 and plate 145). There are some other drawings which are at least inspired by Hellenistic sculptures (see e.g. fig. 63).

III. LEONARDO AS VERROCCHIO'S CO-WORKER

There are no sculptures by Verrocchio which can be dated before Leonardo's apprenticeship; even the "David" cannot be earlier than 1468, the Lavabo of San Lorenzo and the model for the St Thomas of Or San Michele are of about the same time. Different authorities give Leonardo a share in nearly every work which came from Verrocchio's workshop. Malaguzzi Valeri and Cruttwell went very far in this direction. Leonardo is supposed to have assisted in the terracotta relief "Resurrection of Christ" from the Villa Careggi, now in the Bargello, Florence, (according to Valentiner); in the ornamentation of the Lavabo; in the Putto with Dolphin, now at the Palazzo Vecchio; a variant in the (late) Dreyfus collection at Paris, and a terracotta replica in the possession of Conte Francesco Capogrossi Guarna at Rome, ascribed by A. Venturi to Leonardo himself. Mackowsky and Bode thought that the "Lady with Primroses" (plate 148) is by the younger Master. Here some other works have to be added, never thought to be authentic works by Verrocchio but obviously coming from his workshop: the Scipio Relief in the Louvre (No. 668, from the Rattier Collection; see note to plate 5); the two youths with a shield, on the Palazzo Communale of Pistoia, and the two terracotta sketches of angels for the Forteguerri monument (1) at Pistoja, Louvre, (Nos. 815, 816; attribution by Müntz); the so-called Albizzi Madonna in the collection of G. B. Dibblee, Oxford, which is a beautiful replica of the Medici Madonna in the Bargello; a polychromed terracotta Madonna relief in the Metropolitan Museum, New York (Catal. Breck, No. 33; attribution by Seidlitz, 2nd ed., pag. 430: "close to Leonardo"); a St John bust in the Victoria and Albert Museum (fig. 89; attribution by Carotti), and a number of rather different St John busts, including copies in Berlin (2954), the (late) Hainauer Collection (fig. 88) and the (late) Stroganoff Collection (fig. 87; attribution by A. Venturi; but according to Planiscig by Francesco di Giorgio). We may conclude this paragraph with the "Madonna with the laughing Child" in the Victoria and Albert Museum (plate 149), which Sir Claude Phillips, Carotti, Sirén and Valentiner attributed to Leonardo, and of which Sir Kenneth Clark said: "Unlike the other sculpture attributed to Leonardo, this is a charming and distinguished work showing obvious affinities, both of style and spirit, to Leonardo's early drawings".

Most of the sculptures listed in this section have very little to persuade a sceptic.

(1) *The terracotta sketches and the Pistoja coat-of-arms are undoubtedly by Lorenzo di Credi.*

IV. LEONARDO AND FRANCESCO DI GIORGIO

Apart from the St John busts, mentioned in the preceding paragraph, there are five reliefs (1) which are now usually attributed to Francesco di Giorgio (2), but which Bode erroneously ascribed to Leonardo. (Francesco di Giorgio and Leonardo met in 1490; how far did they influence each other? A sheet of Francesco di Giorgio's Treatise of Architecture, c. 1491-1502, at the Ducal Library of Turin, shows the drawing of a diver with exactly the same apparatus as in a sketch of c. 1500 by Leonardo in the *Codice Atlantico*).

A plaquette (3) with the inscription "Chimera" was by G. F. Hill attributed to Francesco di Giorgio; and by Valentiner to Leonardo's workshop. J. B. Venturi (1797) mentioned a relief of St Jerome in the desert, then in the Hugford Collection, Florence, as a work of Leonardo. This relief is perhaps identical with one in the Widener Collection, Elkins Park, Pa., once attributed to Donatello and Desiderio, and now with better reasons to Francesco di Giorgio.

(1) *The deploration of Christ, Carmine, Venice; The Scourging of Christ, Pinacoteca, Perugia; The Judgment of Paris, Duveen, New York, from Dreyfus Collection; Mythological Scene, Berlin, No. 1574; The Allegory of Discord, Victoria and Albert Museum.*
(2) *The suggestion by Seidlitz that they might be by the young Bramante is, I think, tempting. (Seidlitz, 2nd ed., p. 430.)*
(3) *Molinier 495; Victoria and Albert Museum, and Berlin Museum; and the medal in the British Museum (Armand II, No. 29).*

V. LEONARDO AND RUSTICI

See note 54 to Vasari's "Life", pag. 13 of this book; also fig. 19 and plate 150.

Fig. 91. Sketch for the bust of a Christ Child, red chalk, Windsor (12519).

VI. BRONZES OF HORSEMEN AND HORSES

The best of all the known examples is the one in the Budapest Museum (plate 147), which was probably done in imitation of a wax model by Leonardo (see figs. 85 and 90).

A small bronze figure of a man, covering himself with his shield, in the Collection of Principe Trivulzio in Milan, belonged originally either to this or to a similar bronze group. There are other fine bronzes of rearing and of pacing horses, in the Metropolitan Museum, New York, the Frick Collection, the Rijksmuseum, Amsterdam, the Berlin Museum, the Paget Collection, London, the Bargello, the Castello Sforzesco, the Wallace Collection, the British Museum, the Jeannerat Collection, London, and in the Collection of Duchessa dell'Arcuella, Naples. Of other bronzes, which seem to derive from Leonardo's ideas we may mention: a Pegasus in the Ashmolean Museum; a Negro Horseman, fighting a Lion, in the Pennsylvania Museum, Philadelphia, from the Foulc Collection in Paris; a Teodoro Trivulzio on horseback, in the Collection of G. von Benda, Vienna. (Some of the bronzes are close to the works of Bertoldo.)

VII. OTHER ATTRIBUTIONS

Here is a selection taken from the numerous sculptures which were from time to time ascribed to the Master. R. Stites went furthest (Art Studies, 1931), even attributing works of the Master of the Unruly Children to Leonardo. C. Venturi pronounced in favour of a David Relief in the Collection of Count Lanckoronski, Vienna. Three works in wax, which possess very little to recommend them, are still under Leonardo's name: the Flora of the Berlin Museum, the bust of a girl in Lille, and a small horse in Florence (reprod. Suida, 75). R. Stites established a close link between a bronze of Neptune's Chariot in the Vienna Museum (ascribed to Sansovino) and Leonardo's Neptune Cartoon (see No. 37); there is a copy of the complete bronze group in the Beit collection, London.

VIII. LEONARDO AS A RESTORER OF ANTIQUE MARBLES

Restorations were executed in Verrocchio's workshop; the Medici paid him for restoring a red marble Marsyas and a number of antique heads. We may assume that Leonardo, at that time an apprentice in Verrocchio's shop, helped with his work.

In December, 1513, Leonardo came to Rome and made his abode and his studio in the Belvedere of the Vatican. In the same year (1) there was found in Rome, near the church Santa Maria della Minerva, the colossal marble group of the "Nile", which was brought to the Belvedere. The group was much damaged and of the sixteen children playing around the reclining River God hardly anything was left but a few legs. This antique group was restored at the Belvedere and all the children added. I reproduce here, as fig. 92, three of them, together with some representations of children drawn by Leonardo (fig. 93-95). I think a comparison of these illustrations will make it clear why I believe that this antique group was restored in Leonardo's studio.

(1) *Catalogue of 1933, Braccio Nuovo*, No. 109.

No. 147. HORSE AND RIDER, BRONZE, BUDAPEST MUSEUM

Once in the possession of a Hungarian sculptor, who formed his collection in Rome, 1818-1824. A list of similar bronzes in Section III of the survey above. See also bibliography, No. 114. Compare figs. 85 and 90, and some sketches of horsemen by Leonardo, for instance pl. 122, or even the riders in the right background of the Adoration of the Kings, pl. 72.

No. 148. LADY WITH PRIMROSES, FLORENCE

Mackowsky was the first to attribute this sculpture to Leonardo. Suida dated it very early, c. 1470-1475. Compare plates 23 and 40. The hands are more delicately shaped, the fingers finer pointed and their movement more full of life than in any of Verrocchio's authenticated sculptures, but the hands are also worked from a separate piece of marble.

No. 149. THE VIRGIN WITH THE LAUGHING CHILD, VICTORIA & ALBERT MUSEUM, No. 4495-1858

The ascription to the young Leonardo was first put forward by Sir Claude Phillips; in more recent times it was supported by Sirén.

The type of the boy is close to the terracotta putto in the collection of Conte Francesco Capogrossi Guarna in Rome; this terracotta putto, being practically a variant of Verrocchio's Putto with Dolphin, has also been ascribed to Leonardo himself by A. Venturi. Bode thought the Virgin with the Laughing Child a work of Desiderio da Settignano.

No. 150. RUSTICI: BATTLE SCENE, FLORENCE

There are similar terracotta groups by Rustici in the Palazzo Vecchio and in two private collections in Florence, and in the Camondo Collection of the Louvre. Most of them have been discussed in full by R. Stites (in Art Studies, 1926-1931). The photograph of the terracotta group, reproduced as plate 150, was taken for me when the sculpture was still in the Brauer Collection.

See note 54, on page 13 of this book, where the different references of Vasari to a collaboration of Leonardo and Rustici are given and explained.

92   93   94   95

Figs. 92-95. The restoration of the antique marble group 'The Nile'; and children drawn by Leonardo. (92) Three of the playing children, detail of 'The Nile', Vatican Museum, Rome. (93) The two Holy Children embracing, pen-and-ink, copied from a Leonardo drawing, Windsor (12564).—(94) The Madonna of the Yarn-winder, copied from a cartoon by Leonardo, Florence, Uffizi.—(95) St. John, detail of Leonardo's 'Madonna of the Rocks', Louvre. (Compare also fig. 61.)

THE REPRODUCTIONS

NOS. 1-35 HEADS AND PORTRAITS

NOS. 36-52 DRAPERIES AND THE HUMAN FIGURE

NOS. 53-58 ALLEGORY AND MYTHOLOGY

NOS. 59-100 RELIGIOUS SUBJECTS

NOS. 101-120 LANDSCAPES AND FLOWERS

NOS. 121-136 HORSES AND OTHER ANIMALS. THE BATTLE OF ANGHIARI

NOS. 137-153 THE BRONZE HORSE

AND OTHER SCULPTURES

MEASUREMENTS IN CENTIMETRES

AN ASTERISK (*) IN FRONT OF THE NUMBER INDICATES THAT THE

REPRODUCTION IS IN THE SAME SIZE AS THE ORIGINAL

* 1. LEONARDO'S SELF-PORTRAIT. RED CHALK, C. 1510-13. TURIN, ROYAL LIBRARY

* 2. PORTRAIT OF FRANCESCO NANI, CALLED
SANSON, MINISTER GENERALIS OF
THE FRANCISCANS. RED CHALK, 1495.
LONDON, VICTORIA AND ALBERT MUSEUM

* 3. PORTRAIT OF A MAN
? MARQUIS FEDERICO GONZAGA.
SILVERPOINT ON PINK PAPER, C. 1482.
WINDSOR CASTLE, ROYAL LIBRARY

4. PORTRAIT OF A MAN IN THREE POSITIONS, ? CESARE BORGIA. RED CHALK, C. 1502. TURIN, ROYAL LIBRARY. (11.1 X 28.5)

* 5. ANTIQUE WARRIOR. SILVERPOINT AND BROWN CHALK ON CREAM-COLOURED PAPER, C. 1475. LONDON, BRITISH MUSEUM

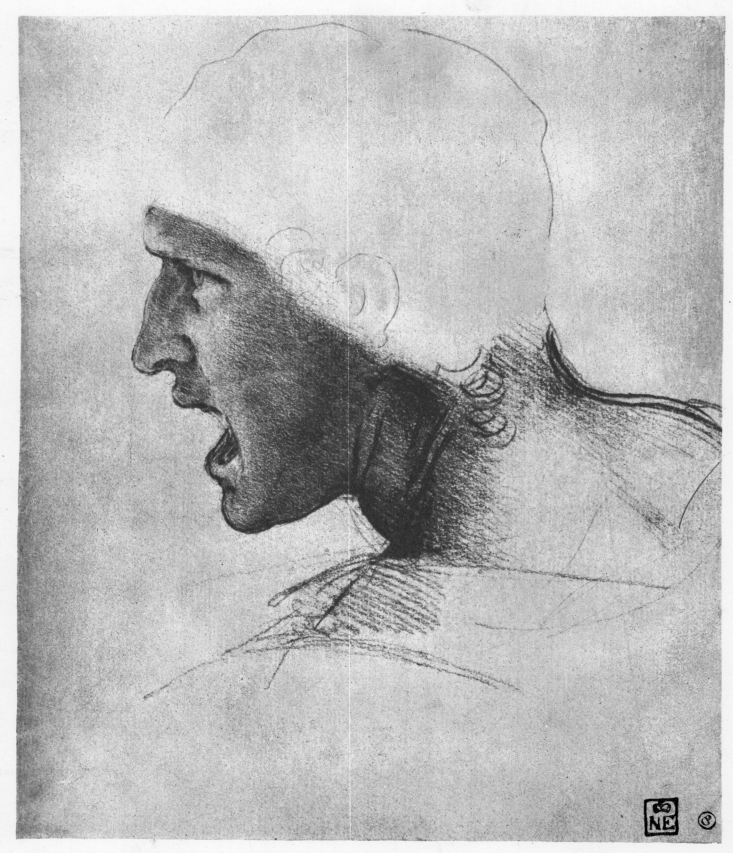

* 6. HEAD OF A WARRIOR (STUDY FOR THE BATTLE OF ANGHIARI). RED CHALK, 1503-05. BUDAPEST, MUSEUM OF FINE ARTS

* 7. HEADS OF WARRIORS (STUDY FOR THE BATTLE OF ANGHIARI).   BLACK CHALK, 1503-05.   BUDAPEST, MUSEUM OF FINE ARTS

8. HEADS OF GIRLS, YOUNG AND OLD MEN. PEN AND INK, C. 1478-80. WINDSOR CASTLE, ROYAL LIBRARY. (40.5 X 29)

* 9. FIVE GROTESQUE HEADS.   PEN AND INK, C. 1490.   WINDSOR CASTLE, ROYAL LIBRARY

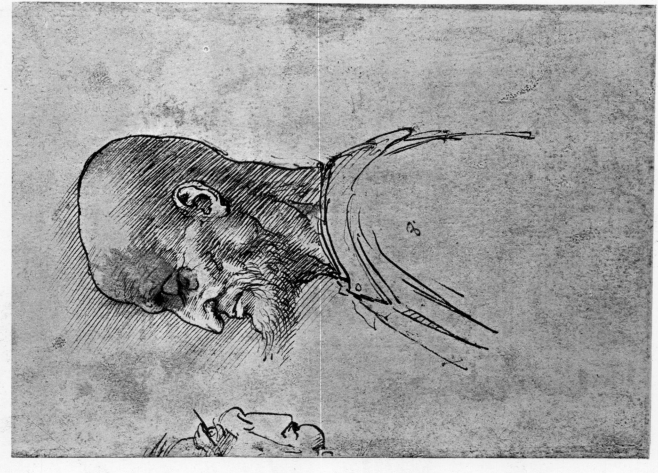

* 11. CARICATURE. PEN AND INK, C. 1490-94

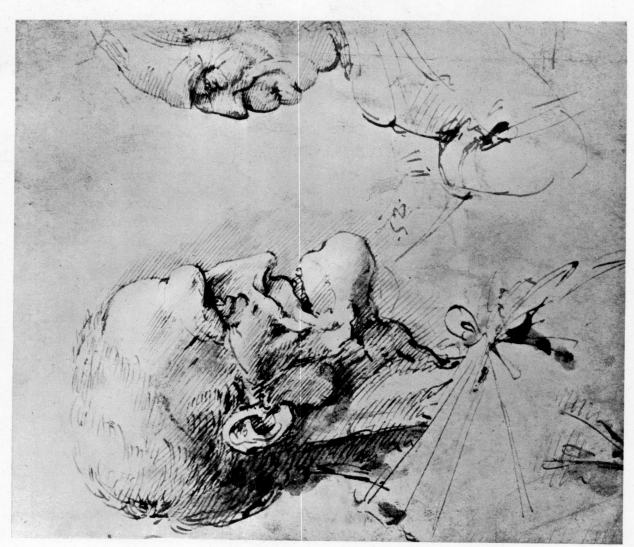

* 10. CARICATURE. PEN AND INK, C. 1495

WINDSOR CASTLE, ROYAL LIBRARY

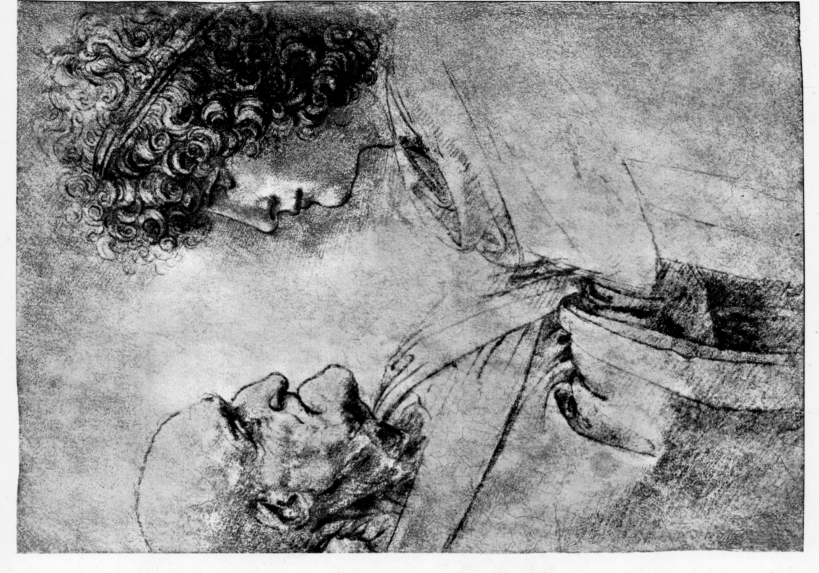

* 13. OLD MAN AND YOUTH. RED CHALK, ABOUT 1495. FLORENCE, UFFIZI

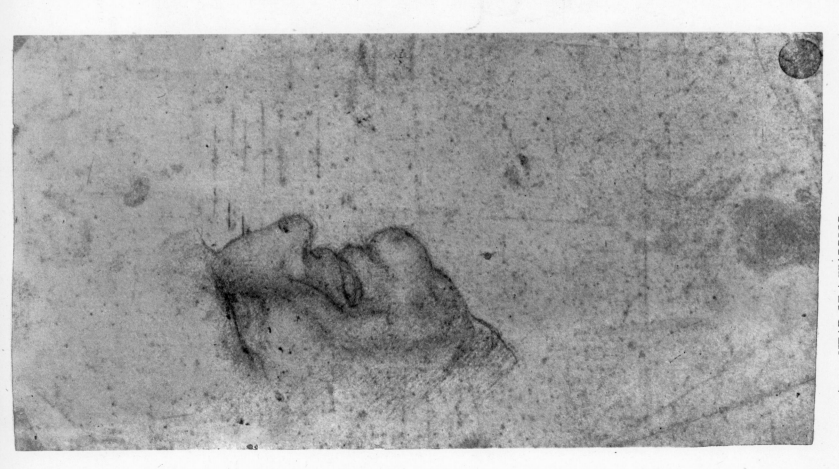

* 12. HEAD OF A WARRIOR. BLACK CHALK, 1503-05. VENICE, ACADEMY

14. CARICATURE. PEN AND BROWN INK, C. 1495-1500. VENICE, ACADEMY. (ENLARGED TO DOUBLE SIZE, ACTUAL SIZE 11.5 x 7.4)

* 15. BALDHEADED OLD MAN. BLACK CHALK ON COARSE-GRAINED GREY PAPER, 1513-16. WINDSOR CASTLE, ROYAL LIBRARY

16. OLD MAN THINKING. PEN AND INK, C. 1510. WINDSOR CASTLE, ROYAL LIBRARY.
(ENLARGED, ACTUAL SIZE 15.2 X 10.7)

* 17.   ST. JAMES THE GREATER (STUDY FOR THE LAST SUPPER).   LOWER LEFT CORNER : THE SFORZA CASTEL AT MILAN.
RED CHALK, AND PEN AND INK, 1495-96.   WINDSOR CASTLE, ROYAL LIBRARY

* 19. ST PHILIP (STUDY FOR THE LAST SUPPER). BLACK CHALK, 1495-96
WINDSOR CASTLE, ROYAL LIBRARY

* 18. ST BARTHOLEMEW (STUDY FOR THE LAST SUPPER). RED CHALK ON RED PAPER, 1495-96
WINDSOR CASTLE, ROYAL LIBRARY

D. 10

* 22. ST ANNE. RED CHALK ON BROWNISH PAPER, TOUCHES OF WHITE AND BLACK, C. 1501. WINDSOR CASTLE, ROYAL LIBRARY

23. PORTRAIT OF GINEVRA DE' BENCI. C. 1474–78. VÏENNA, LIECHTENSTEIN GALLERY. (PANEL, 42 x 37)

24. **SUPPOSED PORTRAIT OF ISABELLA D'ESTE** (1474-1539). BLACK CHALK AND PASTEL, TOUCHES OF RED IN HAIR AND FLESH, YELLOW IN DRESS, 1500. PARIS, LOUVRE. (DETAIL, REDUCED 2 : 3)

* 25. PORTRAIT OF A GIRL WITH A CAP. SILVERPOINT ON PINKISH PAPER, C. 1493–95. WINDSOR CASTLE, ROYAL LIBRARY

26. MONA LISA. 1503. PARIS, LOUVRE. (PANEL, 77 x 53)

27. MONA LISA. DETAIL FROM NO. 26

28. BOLTRAFFIO AND LEONARDO: PORTRAIT OF A LADY, THE SO-CALLED BELLE FERRONNIÈRE. C. 1485–88. PARIS, LOUVRE.
(PANEL, 62 × 44)

29. PORTRAIT OF A LADY WITH AN ERMINE, ? CECILIA GALLERANI. C. 1483. CRACOW, MUSEUM CZARTORYSKI.
(PANEL, 55 X 40.4)

30. PORTRAIT OF A MUSICIAN. C. 1485. UNFINISHED. MILAN, AMBROSIANA. (PANEL, 43 x 31)

31. AMBROGIO DA PREDIS AND LEONARDO : PORTRAIT OF A LADY. C. 1490. MILAN, AMBROSIANA. (PANEL, 51 x 34)

* 32 and * 33. STUDIES FOR THE LEDA. PEN AND INK OVER BLACK CHALK, C. 1506. WINDSOR CASTLE, ROYAL LIBRARY

* 35. STUDY FOR THE ANGEL'S HEAD IN THE VIRGIN OF THE ROCKS.
SILVERPOINT ON PINKISH BROWN PREPARED PAPER, HEIGHTENED WITH WHITE, 1483. TURIN, ROYAL LIBRARY

* 34. STUDY FOR THE HEAD OF ST ANNE.
BLACK CHALK, C. 1508. WINDSOR CASTLE, ROYAL LIBRARY

* 36. DRAPERY OF A PRAYING MADONNA. SILVERPOINT AND BLACK WASH, HEIGHTENED WITH WHITE
ON PINK PREPARED PAPER, C. 1477. ROME, PALAZZO CORSINI

37. DRAPERY OF A SITTING FIGURE. BLACK AND WHITE, WITH THE POINT OF THE BRUSH, ON LINEN, C. 1470-72
FLORENCE, UFFIZI

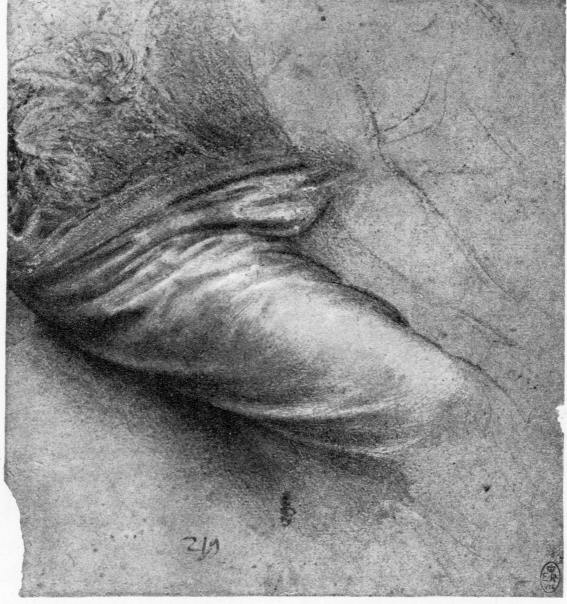

* 38 and * 39. DRAPERY STUDIES FOR THE MADONNA IN THE ST ANNE PAINTING AT THE LOUVRE (CF. NO. 83).
38.—PEN, WASHES OF LAMP BLACK, BLACK CHALK HEIGHTENED WITH WHITE, HAND : RED CHALK, GONE OVER WITH PEN, RED PAPER.
39.—BLACK CHALK, WASHES OF LAMP BLACK, HEIGHTENED WITH WHITE, YELLOWISH PAPER.
C. 1508. WINDSOR CASTLE, ROYAL LIBRARY

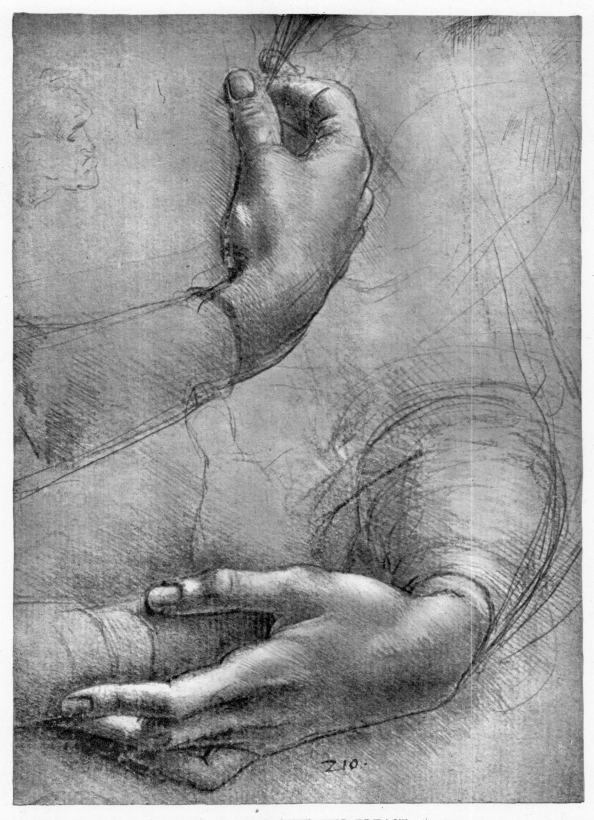

*40. STUDY OF A WOMAN'S HANDS FOLDED OVER HER BREAST. SILVERPOINT, HEIGHTENED WITH WHITE
ON PINK PREPARED PAPER, C. 1478. WINDSOR CASTLE, ROYAL LIBRARY

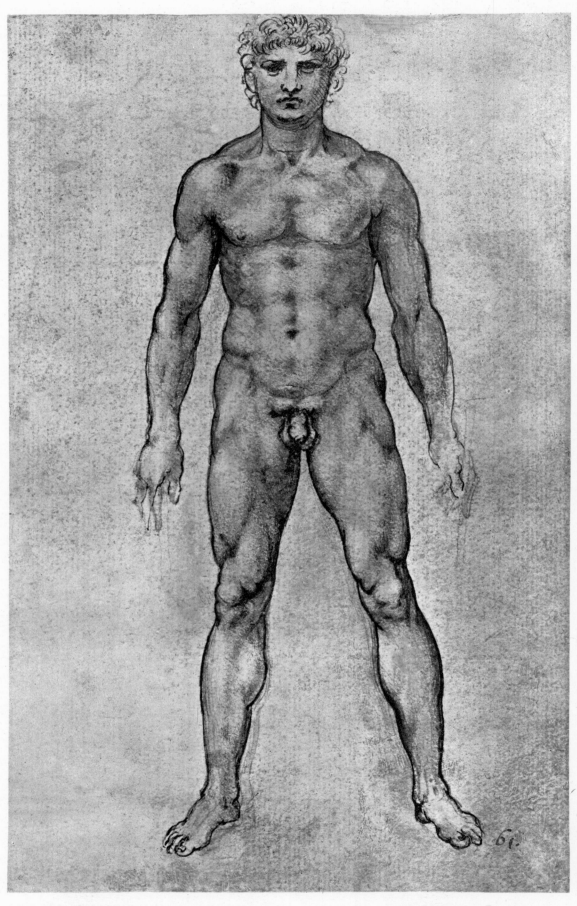

* 41. NUDE FIGURE OF A MAN.   RED CHALK ON RED PAPER, OUTLINES GONE OVER WITH PEN, C. 1503.
WINDSOR CASTLE, ROYAL LIBRARY

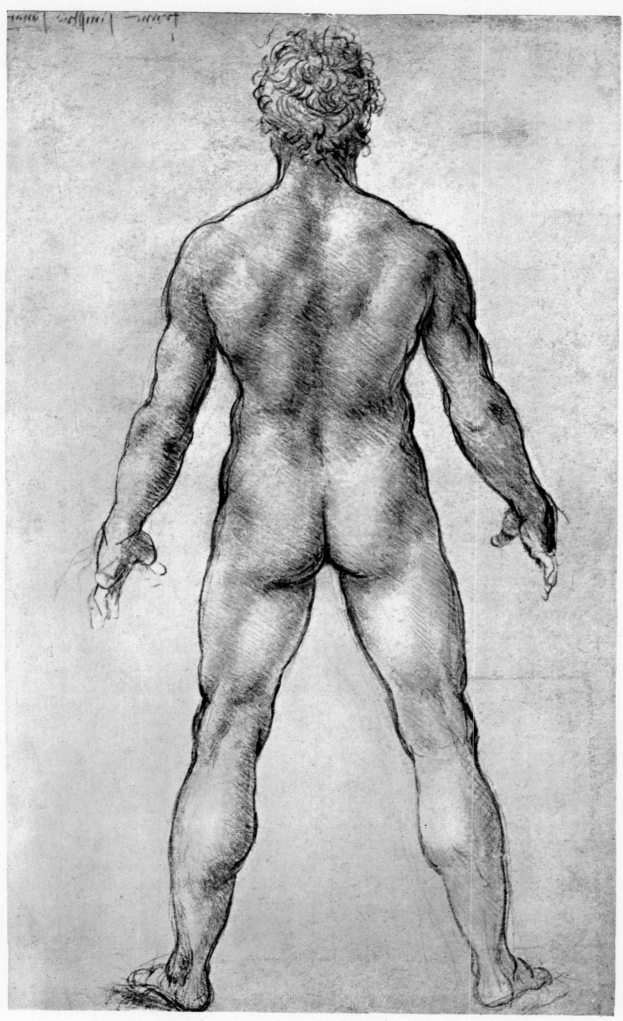

* 42. NUDE FIGURE OF A MAN, HIS BACK TURNED TO THE SPECTATOR. RED CHALK, C. 1503.
WINDSOR CASTLE, ROYAL LIBRARY

* 43. STUDY FOR A ST JOHN THE BAPTIST SEATED, AND AN INFANT ST JOHN WITH LAMB.
BLACK CHALK, C. 1495.   WINDSOR CASTLE, ROYAL LIBRARY

* 44. STUDIES OF THE MOVEMENTS OF
THE HUMAN FIGURE.
RED CHALK, C. 1495.
WINDSOR CASTLE, ROYAL LIBRARY

* 45. STUDY OF THE MOVEMENTS OF
THE HUMAN FIGURE.
RED CHALK, 1495.
LONDON, VICTORIA AND ALBERT MUSEUM

* 46. STUDIES FOR THE BATTLE OF ANGHIARI. PEN AND INK, C. 1503–05. TURIN, ROYAL LIBRARY

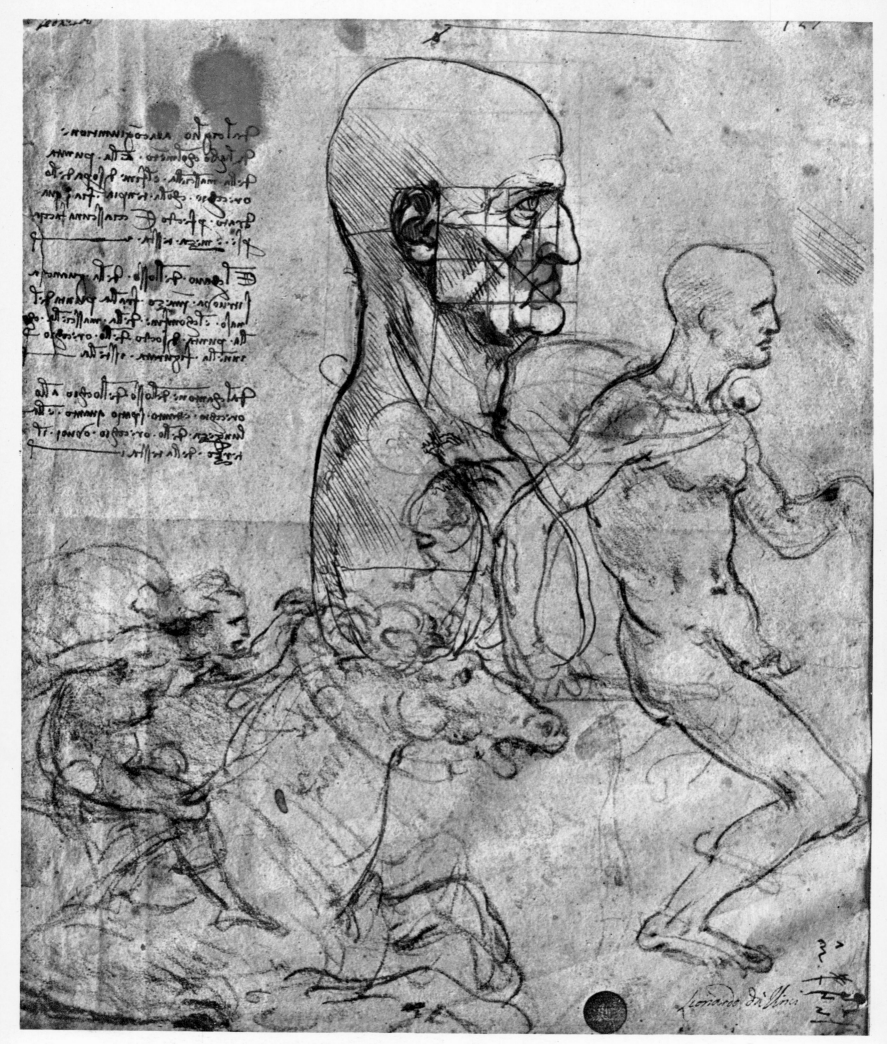

* 47. HEAD MEASURED, AND HORSEMEN. PEN AND INK, C. 1480, AND RED CHALK, C. 1504-06. VENICE ACADEMY

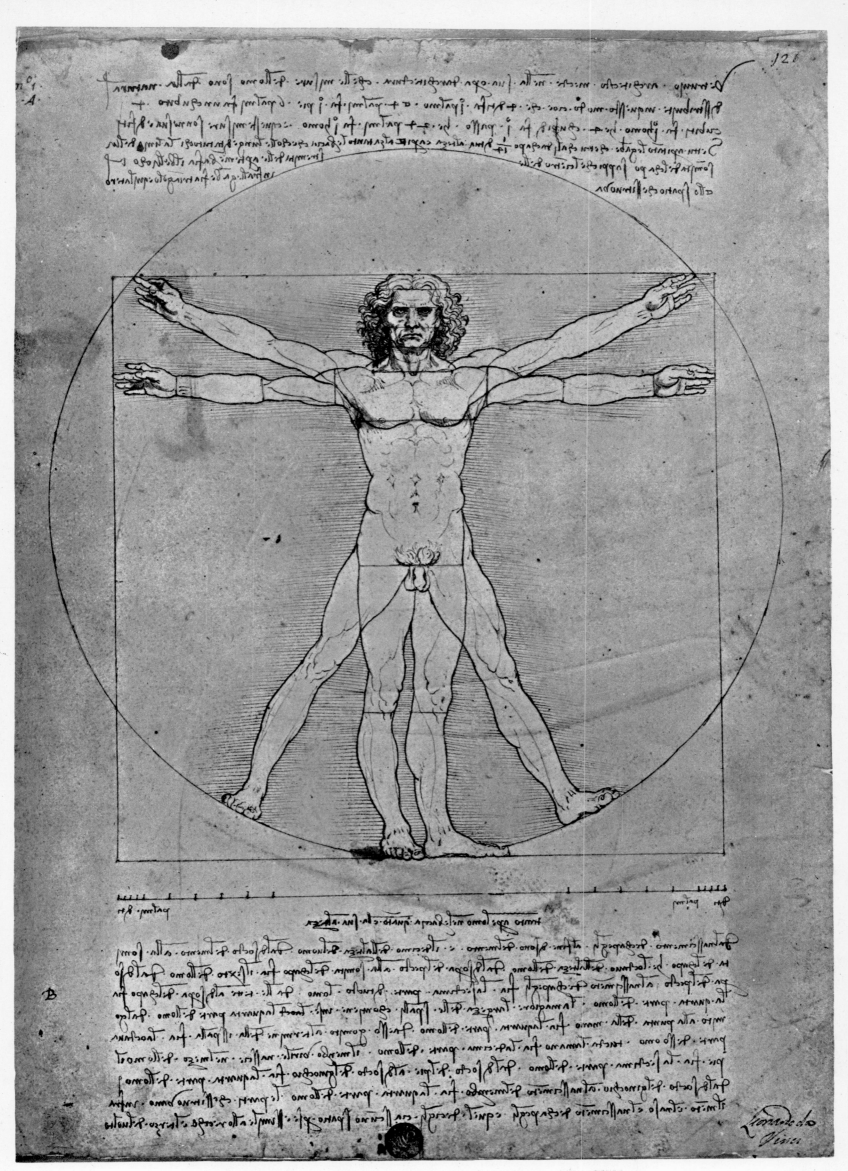

48. THE PROPORTIONS OF THE HUMAN FIGURE, AFTER VITRUVIUS.
PEN AND INK, C. 1492. VENICE, ACADEMY. (34.3 X 24.5)

* 49. HALF-FIGURE OF A WOMAN.   BLACK CHALK, C. 1513.   WINDSOR CASTLE, ROYAL LIBRARY

* 50.   THREE DANCING MAIDENS.   PEN AND INK, C. 1513.   VENICE ACADEMY

* 51. POINTING WOMAN BEHIND A LITTLE WATERFALL. BROWNISH BLACK CHALK, C. 1513.
WINDSOR CASTLE, ROYAL LIBRARY

* 52. YOUTH IN A MASQUERADE COSTUME. PEN AND INK, WASH, OVER BLACK CHALK, C. 1506-07.
WINDSOR CASTLE, ROYAL LIBRARY

* 53. ALLEGORY OF THE LIZARD. PEN AND INK, C. 1495.
NEW YORK, METROPOLITAN MUSEUM OF ART

* 54. ALLEGORY OF THE MIRROR AND THE FIGHTING ANIMALS.
PEN AND INK, C. 1492–94. PARIS, LOUVRE

55. POLITICAL ALLEGORY. PEN AND INK, C. 1483–85. OXFORD, CHRIST CHURCH LIBRARY. (20.5 x 28.5)

57. NEPTUNE. BLACK CHALK, C. 1504. WINDSOR CASTLE, ROYAL LIBRARY. (25.1 X 39.2)

* 58. ALLEGORY OF FORTUNA. SILVERPOINT, PEN AND INK, AND WASH, C. 1483. LONDON, BRITISH MUSEUM

59. **MADONNA WITH THE FRUIT-PLATE.**   SILVERPOINT, PEN AND INK, AND WASH, C. 1480-82.
PARIS, LOUVRE (33×25)

*60. MADONNA WITH THE STOOL. PEN AND INK, AND WASH, ON GREY PAPER, C. 1475–78. FLORENCE, UFFIZI

*61. MADONNA WITH THE UNICORN. PEN AND INK, C. 1478. LONDON, BRITISH MUSEUM

*62 and *62A. STUDIES FOR A VIRGIN AND CHILD WITH A CAT. PEN AND INK, AND WASH, C. 1478–80. LONDON, BRITISH MUSEUM

63. KNEELING MADONNA WITH THE CHILD AND ST JOHN. PEN AND INK, C. 1478–80.
WINDSOR CASTLE, ROYAL LIBRARY. (40.5 X 29)

* 64 and * 64A. STUDIES FOR A MADONNA WITH THE FLOWER.
PEN AND INK, C. 1478. LONDON, BRITISH MUSEUM

65. MADONNA BENOIS. C. 1478–80. LENINGRAD, HERMITAGE. (CANVAS, TRANSFERRED FROM PANEL, 49 X 31.5)

66. THE ANNUNCIATION. C. 1474. FLORENCE, UFFIZI. (PANEL, 98 X 217)

67. ANGEL. DETAIL FROM NO. 66

68. ASCRIBED TO LEONARDO: MADONNA WITH THE CARNATION. C. 1477–78.
MUNICH, AELTERE PINAKOTHEK. (PANEL, 62 x 47)

* 69. STUDY FOR THE HEAD OF A MADONNA. SILVERPOINT ON GREENISH PREPARED PAPER, C. 1484–86.
PARIS, LOUVRE

70. WORKSHOP OF LEONARDO: MADONNA LITTA. C. 1485–90. LENINGRAD, HERMITAGE.
(CANVAS, TRANSFERRED FROM PANEL, 42 × 33)

* 71. STUDY FOR THE ADORATION OF THE KINGS. PEN AND INK, C. 1480. PARIS, LOUVRE

72. ADORATION OF THE KINGS. 1481–82. UNFINISHED. FLORENCE, UFFIZI. (PANEL, 246 × 243)

73. DETAIL FROM No. 72

74. DETAIL FROM No. 72

* 76. STUDY FOR THE BACKGROUND OF THE ADORATION OF THE KINGS. PEN AND INK OVER SILVERPOINT ON PINKISH PREPARED PAPER, C. 1481. FLORENCE, UFFIZI

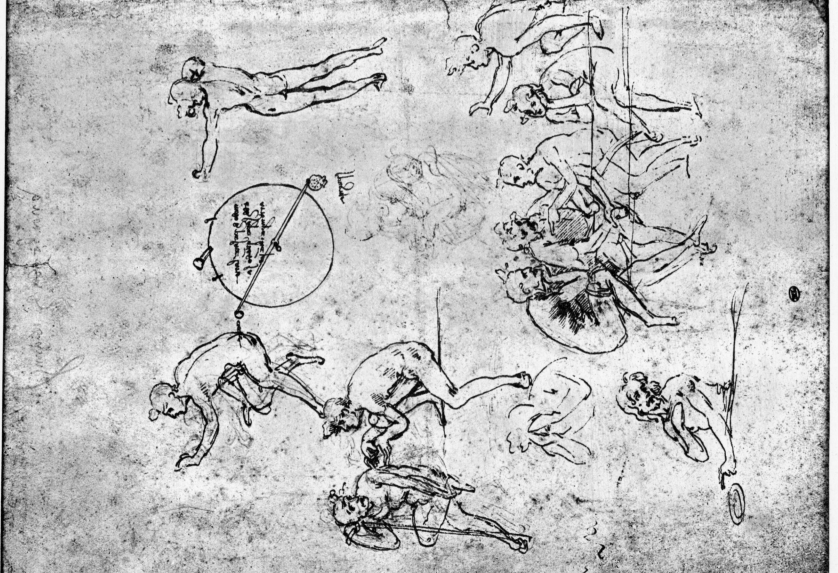

77. STUDY FOR THE ADORATION OF THE SHEPHERDS, FOR THE LAST SUPPER, AND SKETCH OF A HYGROMETER. PEN AND INK OVER SILVERPOINT, C. 1478–80. PARIS, LOUVRE. (27.8 x 20.8)

* 78. STUDY FOR THE ADORATION OF THE SHEPHERDS. PEN AND INK OVER SILVERPOINT, C. 1478–80. BAYONNE, MUSÉE BONNAT

* 80. STUDY FOR THE ADORATION OF THE SHEPHERDS. PEN AND INK OVER SILVERPOINT, C. 1478–80. PARIS, LOUVRE

* 81. STUDIES FOR THE ADORATION OF THE CHILD. PEN AND INK OVER SILVERPOINT ON PINKISH PAPER, C. 1483.
NEW YORK, METROPOLITAN MUSEUM OF ART

* 82. STUDY FOR THE ADORATION OF THE CHILD. PEN AND INK OVER SILVERPOINT, C. 1478-80. VENICE, ACADEMY

83. MADONNA OF THE ROCKS. 1483–90. PARIS, LOUVRE. (CANVAS, TRANSFERRED FROM PANEL, 198 × 123)

84. LEONARDO AND PUPILS: MADONNA OF THE ROCKS. 1506-08. LONDON, NATIONAL GALLERY. (PANEL, 189 x 120)

85. DETAIL FROM No. 83

86. DETAIL FROM No. 83

87. LEONARDO AND PUPILS: VIRGIN AND CHILD WITH ST ANNE AND THE INFANT ST JOHN.
C. 1506–10. UNFINISHED. PARIS, LOUVRE. (PANEL, 170 × 129)

88. CARTOON FOR THE VIRGIN AND CHILD WITH ST ANNE AND THE INFANT ST JOHN.
CHARCOAL ON BROWN PAPER, HEIGHTENED WITH WHITE, C. 1499. LONDON, BURLINGTON HOUSE (139 x 101)

* 89. STUDY FOR THE VIRGIN AND ST ANNE. PEN AND INK, OVER
BLACK CHALK, C. 1501–04. VENICE, ACADEMY

* 89A. STUDY FOR THE VIRGIN AND ST ANNE. PEN AND INK, OVER BLACK CHALK,
C. 1501–04. PARIS, LOUVRE

90. AFTER LEONARDO: FIRST SKETCH FOR THE LAST SUPPER. RED CHALK, C. 1495. VENICE, ACADEMY. (26 X 39)

90A. RECONSTRUCTION OF THE COMPOSITION IN ITS ORIGINAL SHAPE, CF. NO. 90

93.   THE LAST SUPPER.   WALL-PAINTING IN OIL TEMPERA, 1495–98.   MILAN, REFECTORY OF SANTA MARIA DELLE GRAZIE.   (420 × 910)

94. CHRIST. DETAIL FROM NO. 93

95. THE APOSTLES ST BARTHOLOMEW, ST JAMES THE LESS, AND ST ANDREW. DETAIL FROM NO. 93

96. THE APOSTLES ST THOMAS, ST JAMES THE GREAT, AND ST PHILIP. DETAIL FROM NO. 93

97. ST JEROME. C. 1483. UNFINISHED. ROME, VATICAN GALLERY (PANEL, 103 X 75)

98. HEAD OF ST JEROME. DETAIL OF NO. 97

* 99. ST JOHN THE BAPTIST. SILVERPOINT, HEIGHTENED WITH WHITE
ON BLUE PREPARED PAPER, C. 1478. WINDSOR CASTLE, ROYAL LIBRARY

100. ST JOHN THE BAPTIST. C. 1509–12. PARIS, LOUVRE. (PANEL, 69 X 57)

* 101. COURTYARD OF A FOUNDRY. PEN AND INK OVER SILVERPOINT ON BROWNISH PAPER, C. 1487.
WINDSOR CASTLE, ROYAL LIBRARY

* 102. COPSE OF BIRCHES. RED CHALK, C. 1503–05. WINDSOR CASTLE, ROYAL LIBRARY

* 103. RIVER LANDSCAPE. PEN AND INK ON YELLOWISH PAPER, C. 1503–05. WINDSOR CASTLE, ROYAL LIBRARY

* 104. BIRD'S-EYE-VIEW WITH A FERRY-BOAT. PEN AND INK ON YELLOWISH PAPER,
C. 1503–05. WINDSOR CASTLE, ROYAL LIBRARY

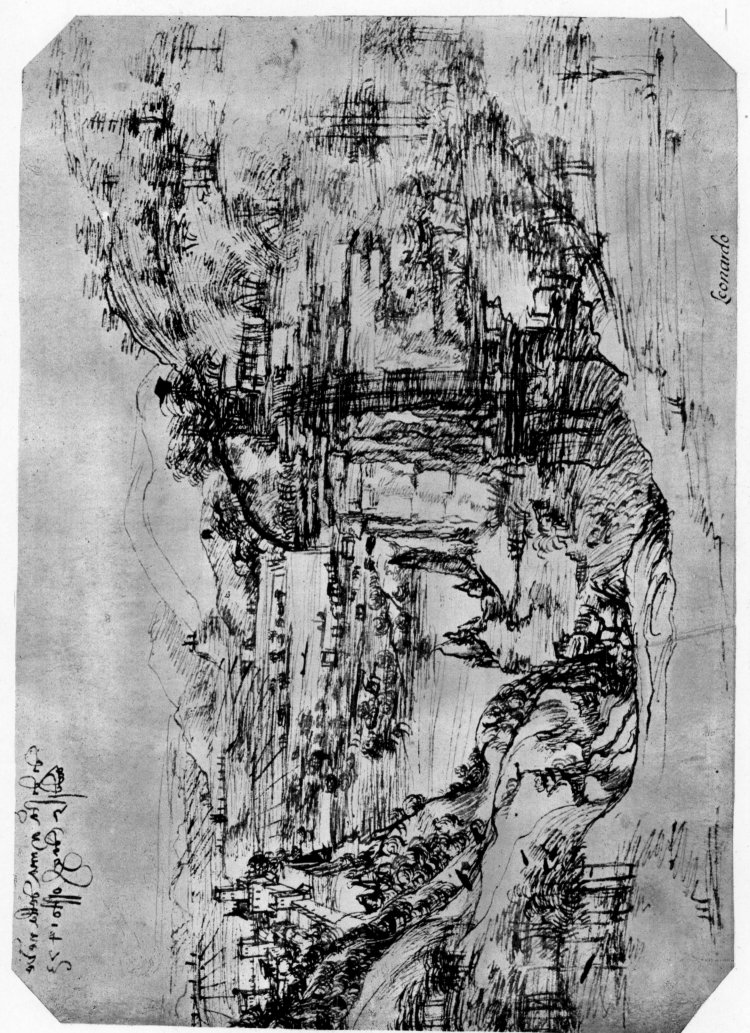

Leonardo

* 105. ARNO LANDSCAPE. PEN AND INK, 1473. FLORENCE, UFFIZI

106. THE DELUGE, WITH NEPTUNE AND THE GODS OF THE WINDS. BLACK CHALK, GONE OVER WITH PEN AND INK, ON GREY PAPER, C. 1514. WINDSOR CASTLE, ROYAL LIBRARY. (27 X 40.8)

* 107. RAVINE WITH WATER-BIRDS. PEN AND INK ON PINKISH PAPER, C. 1478-80. WINDSOR CASTLE, ROYAL LIBRARY

* 108. STORM IN THE ALPS. RED CHALK, C. 1503-05. WINDSOR CASTLE, ROYAL LIBRARY

109. STORM AT AN ENCLOSED BAY. PEN AND INK OVER BLACK CHALK, C. 1512-14.
WINDSOR CASTLE, ROYAL LIBRARY. (16.3 X 20.6)

* 110. DELUGE. DETAIL FROM NO. 106

111. THE BEGINNING OF THE DELUGE. PEN AND INK, AND BROWN WASH OVER BLACK CHALK ON COARSE PAPER, C. 1514-16.
WINDSOR CASTLE, ROYAL LIBRARY.   (15.7 × 20.3)

112. THE DELUGE. BLACK CHALK, C. 1514-16. WINDSOR CASTLE, ROYAL LIBRARY. (15.8 × 20.3)

* 113. STUDIES OF FLOWERS.   PEN AND INK ON CREAM COLOURED PAPER, C. 1481.   VENICE, ACADEMY

116 and 117. BRANCHES OF BLACKBERRY. RED CHALK ON PINK PREPARED PAPER, C. 1503.
WINDSOR CASTLE, ROYAL LIBRARY. (18.8 x 16.5 and 15.5 x 16.2)

118. STAR OF BETHLEHEM AND OTHER PLANTS.   PEN AND INK OVER RED CHALK, C. 1506.
WINDSOR CASTLE, ROYAL LIBRARY.   (19.8 x 16)

119. STUDY OF A PLANT.   PEN AND INK OVER FAINT BLACK CHALK, C. 1506.
WINDSOR CASTLE, ROYAL LIBRARY.   (21.2 x 22.9)

120. **CESARE DA SESTO AND LEONARDO: STUDY OF A TREE.** PEN AND INK OVER BLACK CHALK, ON BLUE PAPER, C. 1503
WINDSOR CASTLE, ROYAL LIBRARY. (39.2 x 26.5)

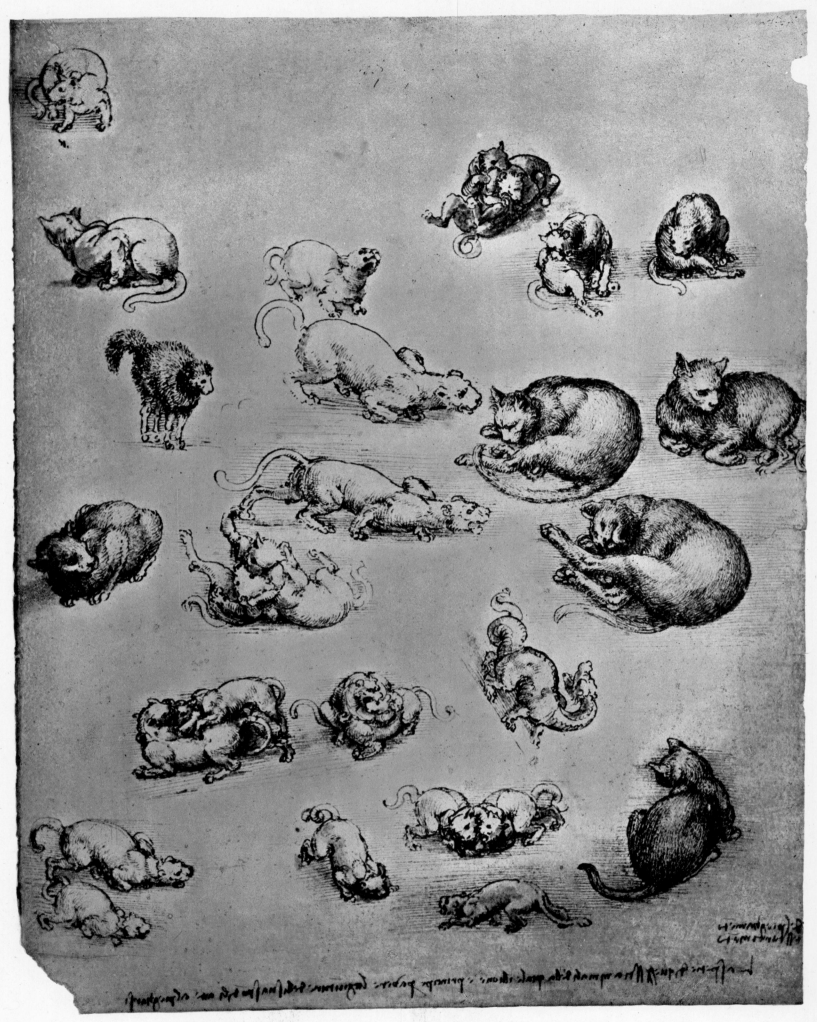

* 121. STUDIES OF CATS. PEN AND INK OVER BLACK CHALK, C. 1506. WINDSOR CASTLE, ROYAL LIBRARY

* 122.   STUDIES OF ST GEORGE AND THE DRAGON.   PEN AND INK, C. 1506.   WINDSOR CASTLE, ROYAL LIBRARY

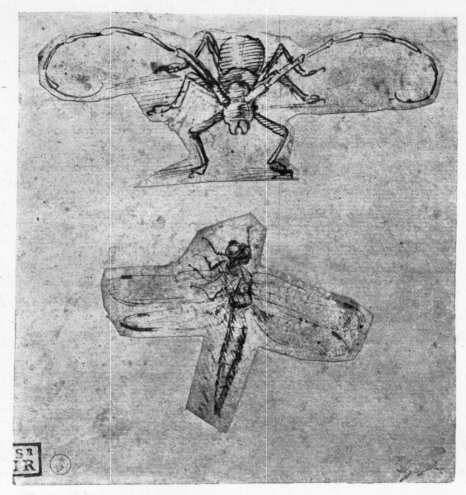

* 123. BEETLE AND DRAGON-FLY. PEN AND INK ON PINK PAPER, C. 1485–90.
TURIN, ROYAL LIBRARY

* 124. ASSES AND OX. SILVERPOINT, PEN AND INK, C. 1480. WINDSOR CASTLE, ROYAL LIBRARY

125. HEADS OF HORSES. (FOR THE ADORATION OF THE KINGS, CF. NO. 72).
SILVERPOINT ON BUFF PREPARED PAPER, 1480–81. DETAIL.
WINDSOR CASTLE, ROYAL LIBRARY. (14.9 WIDE)

* 126. HEAD OF A HORSE.
PEN AND INK, WASH, 1481–82.
WINDSOR CASTLE, ROYAL LIBRARY

127. HORSES AND HORSEMEN. DETAIL FROM THE ADORATION OF THE KINGS, CF. NO. 72. 1481–82. FLORENCE, UFFIZI

* 128. HORSEMAN, FOR THE ADORATION OF THE KINGS, CF. NO. 72.
PEN AND INK OVER SILVERPOINT ON BUFF PAPER, 1480–81.
LONDON, CAPTAIN NORMAN R. COLVILLE

* 128a. HORSEMAN, FOR THE ADORATION OF THE KINGS, CF. NO. 72
SILVERPOINT ON PREPARED PAPER, 1480–81.
PROVIDENCE, RHODE ISLAND, U.S.A., JOHN NICHOLAS BROWN

129. HORSES, LION'S HEAD, AND FACE OF A MAN. STUDIES FOR THE BATTLE OF ANGHIARI. PEN AND INK, C. 1504.
WINDSOR CASTLE, ROYAL LIBRARY. (19.6 x 30.8)

* 130. **HORSE REARING.** STUDY FOR THE BATTLE OF ANGHIARI.
RED CHALK, C. 1504. WINDSOR CASTLE, ROYAL LIBRARY

131. **HORSEMEN AND FOOT-SOLDIERS.** STUDIES FOR THE BATTLE OF ANGHIARI. RED CHALK, C. 1504.
WINDSOR CASTLE, ROYAL LIBRARY. (16.8 x 24)

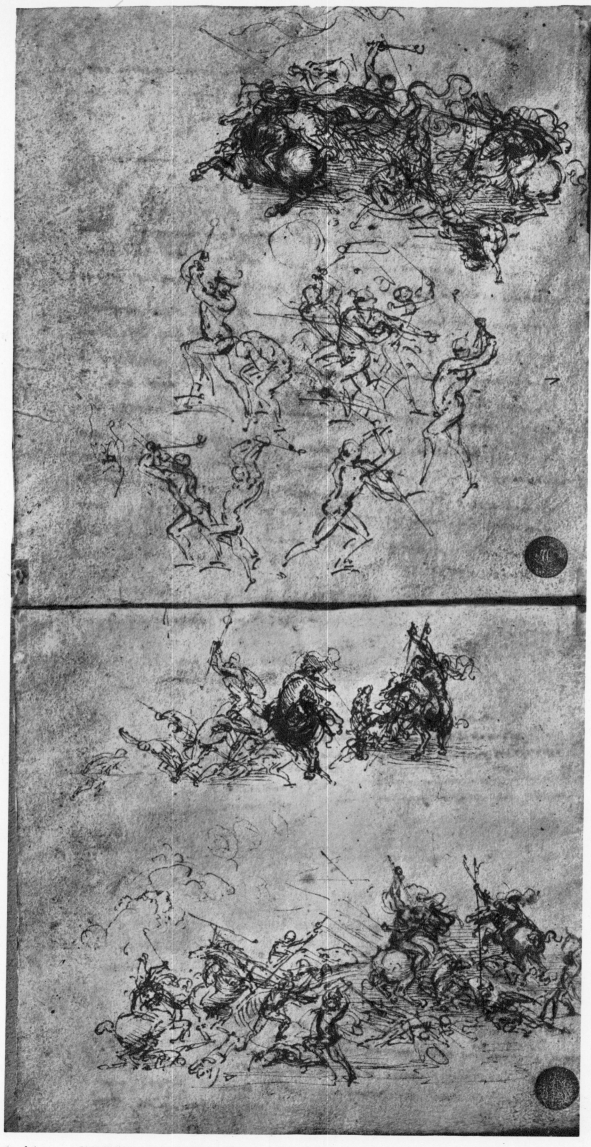

* 132 and * 133. STUDIES FOR THE BATTLE OF ANGHIARI. PEN AND INK, C. 1503. VENICE, ACADEMY

* 134. STUDY FOR THE BATTLE OF ANGHIARI. PEN AND INK, C. 1503. LONDON, BRITISH MUSEUM

* 135. STUDY FOR THE BATTLE OF ANGHIARI. (CENTRAL PART : THE FIGHT FOR THE STANDARD.)
PEN AND INK, C. 1503. VENICE, ACADEMY

* 136. STUDIES FOR THE BATTLE OF ANGHIARI (CLOSE FIGHTING OF TWO SOLDIERS). PEN AND INK, C. 1503. VENICE, ACADEMY

* 137. STUDY FOR THE TRIVULZIO MONUMENT. RED CHALK, PEN AND INK, C. 1511.
WINDSOR CASTLE, ROYAL LIBRARY

2

*138. STUDY FOR THE SFORZA MONUMENT. SILVERPOINT ON BLUE PREPARED PAPER, C. 1488-90. WINDSOR CASTLE, ROYAL LIBRARY

139-141. SKETCHES IN PREPARATION OF CASTING THE BRONZE HORSE FOR THE SFORZA MONUMENT. 1491-93.
(139.—THE MODEL PACKED FOR TRANSPORT. RED CHALK DRAWING IN THE CODEX ATLANTICUS.
140.—HORSE WITHIN A MOULD. DETAIL OF A PEN AND INK DRAWING, WINDSOR.
141. TWO SKETCHES OF MOULDS FOR CASTING A PRANCING HORSE. DETAIL OF A PEN AND INK DRAWING, WINDSOR)

* 146. STUDIES FOR THE TRIVULZIO MONUMENT. PEN AND BISTRE ON COARSE GREYISH PAPER, C. 1511.
WINDSOR CASTLE, ROYAL LIBRARY

147. LEONARDO'S WORKSHOP: HORSE AND RIDER. BRONZE, ? C. 1506–08. BUDAPEST, MUSEUM OF FINE ARTS. (23.5 HIGH)

148. VERROCCHIO'S WORKSHOP (ASCRIBED TO LEONARDO): LADY WITH PRIMROSES. MARBLE, C. 1478-80.
FLORENCE, BARGELLO (65 HIGH)

149. VERROCCHIO'S WORKSHOP (ASCRIBED TO LEONARDO): THE VIRGIN WITH THE LAUGHING CHILD.
TERRACOTTA, C. 1475–78. LONDON, VICTORIA AND ALBERT MUSEUM. (48.5 HIGH)

150. GIAN FRANCESCO RUSTICI (WITH THE HELP OF LEONARDO?): BATTLE SCENE.
TERRACOTTA, C. 1508. FLORENCE, BARGELLO (45.5 HIGH)

INDEX OF COLLECTIONS

SHORT BIBLIOGRAPHY

THIS LIST CONTAINS ONLY BOOKS ON LEONARDO AS AN ARTIST

BIBLIOGRAPHY

(1) *Raccolta Vinciana presso l' Archivio Storico del Commune di Milano*, ed. Ettore Verga, since 1905.

(2) Ettore Verga, *Bibliografia Vinciana*, 1493-1930. Bologna 1931 (2 vols.).

A good bibliography will be found in Poggi's edition of Vasari (No. 26 of this list); also in Pauli's article in *Thieme's Lexikon*, vol. XXIII.

THE MANUSCRIPTS

A list of all publications of Leonardo's MSS. in Richter, II, pp. 419-421. (See No. 6.)

(3) E. Solmi, *Le fonti dei manoscritti di L. da V.* Turin 1908.

(4) Gerolamo Calvi, *I Manoscritti di Leonardo da Vinci dal punto di vista cronologico storico e biografico*. Bologna 1925.

(5) Edward McCurdy, *L. da V.'s Note-Books*. London 1906. (New edition, in 2 vols., London 1938.)

(6) *The Literary Works of Leonardo da Vinci*. Compiled and edited from the original manuscripts by Jean Paul Richter. Second edition enlarged and revised. 2 vols. Oxford University Press, London and New York 1939.

LEONARDO'S TREATISE ON PAINTING

(7) *Il Trattato della Pittura* : Bibliography 1651-1913, by Aldo Mieli, in *Archivio di storia della scienza* I, 1919-20, p. 177 et seq.

(8) *Trattato della Pittura di Leonardo da Vinci*, Prefazione di Angelo Borzello. Lanciano 1914. (The first edition of Leonardo's Trattato was issued in Paris, 1651.)

(9) *Trattato della Pittura*, Italian edition of the Cod. Urbinas 1270 in the Vatican, with German translation in *Quellenschriften für Kunstgeschichte*, ed. Heinrich Ludwig, 3 vols. Vienna 1882. (Second edition by Marie Herzfeld, Jena 1909.) Additions : *Das Buch von der Malerei, Neues Material*, ed. H. Ludwig. Stuttgart 1885.

(10) *A Treatise on Painting*. An English translation of Leonardo's *Trattato della Pittura*, by John Francis Rigaud. London 1877.

(11) Lionello Venturi, *La Critica e l' Arte di Leonardo da Vinci*. Bologna 1919.

THE DOCUMENTS

(12) Francesco Albertini : *Memoriale di molte statue e pitture della Città di Firenze*. Florence 1510. (Mentions Verrocchio's "Baptism of Christ" in San Salvi, containing *"un angelo di Leonardo Vinci"*. It also refers to the Anghiari cartoon, etc.)

(13) Carlo Amoretti, *Memorie storiche sulla vita. . .de Leonardo da Vinci*. Milan 1804.

(14) G. Campori, *Nuovi documenti per la vita di Leonardo da Vinci*. Modena 1865.

(15) G. Milanesi, *Documenti inediti riguardanti Leonardo da Vinci*. Florence 1872.

(16) G. Uzielli, *Ricerche intorno a Leonardo da Vinci* : vol. I, Florence 1872 (second edition, Turin 1896). vol. II, Rome 1884.

(17) N. Smiraglia Scognamiglio, *Ricerche e documenti sulla giovinezza di Leonardo da Vinci*. Naples 1900.

(18) C. Brun, *Die Quellen zur Biographie Leonardos*, in *Festgabe für Hugo Blümner*, Zurich 1914.

(19) G. Calvi, *Contributi alla Biografia di Leonardo da Vinci*, in *Archivio Storico Lombardo*, 1916, XLIII.

(20) Luca Beltrami, *Documenti e Memorie riguardanti la vita e le opere di Leonardo da Vinci*. Milan 1919.

Many documents are reprinted in the notes to the Vasari editions by Milanesi, Horne and Poggi (Nos. 24-26). A useful survey, by W. v. Seidlitz, *Regesten zum Leben Leonardos da Vinci*, in *Repertorium f. Kunstwissenschaft* XXXIV, 1911, pp. 448-458.

THE EARLY BIOGRAPHIES

(21) *Libro di Antonio Billi*, ed. Carl Frey, Berlin 1892. (The earliest life among the Florentine art annalists, named after the merchant who was either the author or the possessor of the book, written about 1516.)

(22) Paolo Giovio, *The Life of Leonardo da Vinci*, in Richter I, pp. 2-3, Oxford 1939. (Written c. 1527-30.) Cf. No. 6.

(23) *Anonimo Magliabecchiano (or Gaddiano)*, ed. Carl Frey, Berlin 1892 (Written between 1540-48, derived information from Billi's book and served as a source for Vasari.)

(24) Giorgio Vasari, *Opere, con nuove annotazioni e commenti di Gaetano Milanesi*. Florence 1882-1906. (First edition of Vasari's book 1550, second edition 1568.)

(25) *The Life of Leonardo da Vinci by Giorgio Vasari*, done into English with a commentary by Herbert Horne. London 1903.

(26) Giovanni Poggi, *Leonardo da Vinci, La Vita di Giorgio Vasari nuovamente commentata e illustrata*. Florence 1919 (200 plates).

(27) Giorgio Vasari, *The Lives of the Painters, Sculptors and Architects*. Translated by A. B. Hinds, 1900. 4 vols. Everyman's Library, London 1927 (vol. II).

(28) Antonio de Beatis, *Die Reise des Kardinals Luigi d'Aragona*, ed. L. Pastor, Freiburg, 1905. (The Cardinal visited Leonardo at Amboise, in October 1517.)

(29) G. Paolo Lomazzo, *Trattato dell' Arte della pittura*. Milan 1584 (English translation, Oxford 1598).

(30) G. Paolo Lomazzo, *Idea del tempio della pittura*. Milan 1590. (Lomazzo had direct information about Leonardo from Francesco Melzi.)

LEONARDO'S APPEARANCE

(31) Luca Beltrami, *Il volto di Leonardo da Vinci*. (Istituto di Studi Vinciani), Rome 1919. (Also in *Emporium*, Bergamo 1919, pp. 3-17.)

(32) Emil Möller, *Wie sah Leonardo aus ?* in *Belvedere*, IX, Vienna 1926, pp. 29-46.

(33) L. Planiscig, *Leonardos Porträte und Aristoteles*, in *Festschrift für Julius Schlosser*. Vienna 1927.

(34) Giorgio Nicodemi, *Il volto di Leonardo da Vinci*, in *Leonardo da Vinci*, (Mostra, Milan 1939) ed. Istituto Geografico de Agostini, Novara (1939).

REPRODUCTIONS

(35) Luca Pacioli, *De Divina Proportione*, Venice 1509 (Illustrations by Leonardo da Vinci).

(36) Carlo Giuseppi Gerli, *Desegni di Leonardo da Vinci incisi e publ.* Milan 1734.

(37) Anny A. Popp, *Leonardo da Vinci : Zeichnungen*. München 1928.

(38) *I disegni di Leonardo da Vinci*. Published in facsimile by the R. Commissione Vinciana (A. Venturi). Part I-IV. Rome 1928-36.

(39) Heinrich Bodmer, *Leonardo : des Meisters Gemälde und Zeichnungen*. Klassiker der Kunst, vol. 37. Stuttgart 1931.

(40) H. Bodmer, *Disegni di Leonardo*. Florence 1939.

(41) Giorgio Nicodemi, Leonardo da Vinci : *Gemälde, Zeichnungen, Studien*. Zurich 1939. (A good introduction and bibliography by the Director of the Museo di Castello Sforzesco in Milan, but poor reproductions, including some of drawings not by Leonardo.)

(42) Bernhard Berenson, *The Drawings of the Florentine Painters*, Amplified Edition, 3 vols. Chicago 1938.

Most of the volumes mentioned above contain not only good reproductions but also introductions and notes of the highest value. Publications of scientific illustrations by Leonardo—on anatomy, mechanics, flight of birds, etc.—are not included in our list, but may be found in Richter II, p. 419 (No. 6).

DRAWINGS IN INDIVIDUAL COLLECTIONS

Florence, Uffizi.

(43) Pasquale Nerino Ferri, *Catalogo riassuntivo della raccolta di disegni antichi e moderni della R. Galleria degli Uffizi di Firenze.* Rome 1890.

(44) Giovanni Poggi, *Drawings by Leonardo da Vinci.* (The drawings of the Royal Gallery of the Uffizi in Florence, published by Leo S. Olschki, fifth series, third portfolio; 20 plates.) Florence 1922.

London, British Museum.

(45) *I manoscritti e i disegni di Leonardo da Vinci, Il Codice Arundel* 263; ed. R. Commissione Vinciana, Rome 1923-30. (Four parts.)

Milan, Ambrosiana.

(46) S. Dozio, *Degli scritti e disegni di Leonardo da Vinci all' Ambrosiana.* Milan 1871.

(47) Giovanni Piumati, *Il Codice Atlantico di Leonardo da Vinci nella Biblioteca Ambrosiana di Milano.* Milan 1894-1904.

(48) L. Beltrami, *Disegni di Leonardo e della sua scuola alla Biblioteca Ambrosiana.* Milan 1904.

Milan, Brera.

(49) Francesco Malaguzzi Valeri, *I disegni della R. Pinacoteca di Brera.* Milan 1906.

Milan 1939, Leonardo Exhibition.

(50) *Catalogo della Mostra di Leonardo da Vinci,* Milan 1939.

(51) Leonardo da Vinci, *Pubblicazione promossa dalla mostra di L. da V., Milano* (Italian and English Edition). Novara 1939.

Paris, Louvre.

(52) L. Demonts, *Les dessins de Leonardo da Vinci au Musée du Louvre.* Paris 1922.

Oxford.

(53) Sidney Colvin, *Drawings of the old Masters in the University Galleries and in the Library of Christ Church, Oxford,* 3 vols. Oxford 1907.

Turin, Royal Library.

(54) Pietro Carlevaris, *I disegni di Leonardo da Vinci della Biblioteca di S. M. di Torino.* Turin 1888.

Venice, Accademia.

(55) Gino Fogolari, *I disegni delle R. Galleria dell' Accademia di Venezia.* Milan 1913.

Windsor Castle.

(56) Sir Kenneth Clark, *A Catalogue of the drawings of Leonardo da Vinci... at Windsor Castle.* Cambridge 1935, 2 vols. (The best critical book on Leonardo's drawings, containing much more than a study of the Windsor drawings).

For Leonardo's paintings in different collections see the museum catalogues.

LEONARDO'S EARLIEST PERIOD

(57) Hans Mackowsky, *Verrocchio.* Leipzig 1901. (Contains several attributions to Leonardo.)

(58) Jens Thiis, *Leonardo da Vinci: The Florentine years of Leonardo and Verrocchio.* London (1913). (Swedish edition 1909; revised French edition 1928.)

(59) Sir Charles Holmes, in *Burlington Magazine,* February 1914, *review of Thiis's book on Leonardo.* (About Leonardo's activities in Verrocchio's workshop.)

(60) W. R. Valentiner, *Leonardo as Verrocchio's co-worker,* in *The Art Bulletin* (XII, 1) University of Chicago, March 1930, pp. 43-89.

(61) W. R. Valentiner, *Leonardo und Desiderio,* in *Jahrb. d. preuss. Kunstsamml.* LXI, 1932, p. 53 et seq.

(62) Bernhard Berenson, *Verrocchio e Leonardo—Leonardo e Credi,* in *Bollettino d'Arte,* 1933-34 (pp. 241-264; 193-213).

(63) Adolfo Venturi, *Leonardo scultore nella bottega del Verrocchio* in *Nuova Antologia,* 1934, March, pp. 34-39; *L'Arte* 1936, pp. 243-265.

(64) W. R. Valentiner, *Über zwei Kompositionen Leonardos,* in *Jahrb. d. preuss. Kunstsamml.,* vol. 56, 1935, p. 213 et seq.

(65) Sigmund Freud, *Eine Kindheitserinnerung des Leonardo da Vinci.* Vienna 1910. (Also an English translation, by Prof. A. A. Brill.)

BIOGRAPHIES AND BOOKS ON LEONARDO'S ART

(66) J. P. Richter, *Leonardo da Vinci.* London 1880.

(67) Giovanni Morelli (Ivan Lermolieff), *Die Werke der italienischen Meister.* Leipzig 1880. (English edition, Italian Painters, 2 vols., London 1892-93.)

(68) Gabriel Séailles, *Léonard de Vinci, L'artiste et le savant.* Paris 1892.

(69) Walter Pater, *The Renaissance.* London 1893 (pp. 103-135: Essay on Leonardo).

(70) Paul Müller-Walde, *Leonardo da Vinci: Lebensskizze und Forschungen.* München 1889-90 (unfinished).

(71) Paul Müller-Walde, *Beiträge zur Kenntnis des Leonardo da Vinci,* in *Jahrbuch der preussischen Kunstsammlungen,* Berlin 1897-99.

(72) Edmondo Solmi, *Leonardo.* Florence 1900.

(73) Georg Gronau, *Leonardo da Vinci.* London 1902.

(74) W. v. Seidlitz, *Leonardo da Vinci, der Wendepunkt der Renaissance,* 2 vols. Berlin 1909. (The second edition, very different from the first, Vienna 1935.)

(75) Bernhard Berenson, *The Study and Criticism of Italian Art,* III. London 1916 (pp. 1-37, Leonardo da Vinci, an attempt at a revaluation).

(76) Osvald Sirén, *Leonardo da Vinci, The Artist and the Man.* New Haven 1916. (Revised French edition, 3 vols., Paris and Brussels 1928. See the review by Sir Eric Maclagan, in *Burlington Magazine* LIV, 1929, p. 277.)

(77) Adolfo Venturi, *Leonardo da Vinci Pittore.* Bologna (1920).

(78) Giulio Carotti, *Leonardo da Vinci.* Turin 1921.

(79) Wilhelm von Bode, *Studien über Leonardo da Vinci.* Berlin 1921.

(80) A. Schiaparelli, *Leonardo rittratista.* Milan 1922.

(81) Ettore Verga, *Gli studi intorno a Leonardo da Vinci.* Rome 1923.

(82) Adolfo Venturi, *Storia dell'Arte Italiana,* vol. IX,i. Milan 1925.

(83) Aldo de Rinaldis, *Storia dell' Opera pittorica di Leonardo da Vinci.* Bologna (1926).

(84) Max Dvořák, *Geschichte der italienischen Kunst im Zeitalter der Renaissance: Akademische Vorlesungen (Vienna,* 1918-20). Munich, 1927 (Vol. I, pp. 143-194: Leonardo.)

(85) Edmund Hildebrandt, *Leonardo da Vinci.* Berlin 1927.

(86) Edward McCurdy, *The mind of Leonardo da Vinci.* London 1928.

(87) Paul Valéry, *Introduction to the method of Leonardo da Vinci,* translated from the French by Thomas McCreevy (1894 and 1919). London 1929.

(88) Wilhelm Suida, *Leonardo und sein Kreis.* München 1929.

(89) Sir Kenneth Clark, *Leonardo da Vinci: An Account of his development as an artist.* Cambridge 1929.

(90) Edward McCurdy, *Leonardo da Vinci: The Artist.* London 1933.

(91) Girolamo Calvi, *Vita di Leonardo da Vinci.* Brescia 1936.

BOOKS ON SINGLE LEONARDO PAINTINGS

(92) *"The Last Supper."* Giuseppe Bossi, *Del 'Cenacolo' di Leonardo da Vinci.* Milan 1810.

(93) Goethe, *Über Leonards da Vinci Abendmahl zu Mailand,* in *Kunst und Alterthum,* III, 1817 (A review of Bossi's book).

(94) J. Strzygowski, *Leonardos Abendmahl und Goethes Deutung,* in *Goethe-Jahrbuch* 1896, p. 138 et seq.

(95) Otto Hoerth, *Das Abendmahl des L. da V.* Leipzig 1907.

(96) Luca Beltrami, *Il Cenacolo di Leonardo.* Milan 1908.

(97) Heinrich Wölfflin, *Die Klassische Kunst*; 1898, 6th ed. Munich 1914 (pp. 23-42: analysis of the composition of four Leonardo paintings—Last Supper, Mona Lisa, St Anne, Battle of Anghiari).

(98) Salomon Reinach, *La Tristesse de Mona Lisa,* in *Bulletin des Musées de France.* Paris 1909.

(99) Luca Beltrami, *Leonardo da Vinci e la Sala delle Asse.* Milan 1902.

(100) M. Lessing, *Die Anghiarischlacht des L. da V.* Bonn 1935.

(101) Carl Justi, *Das Geheimnis der Leonardesken Altargemälde in Valencia,* in *Repert. f. Kunstw.* XVI, 1893.

MISCELLANEA

(102) Luca Beltrami, *La destra mano di Leonardo da Vinci.* Milan (n.d.)

(103) Victor Mortet, *La mésure de la figure humaine et le canon des proportions d'après les dessins de Villard de Honnecourt, d'Albert Dürer et de Léonard de Vinci.* "Melanges Chatelain", Paris 1910.

(104) Hans Klaiber, *Leonardo da Vincis Stellung in der Geschichte der Physiognomik und Mimik,* in *Repertorium f. Kunstwissensch.* XXVIII.

(105) Giambattista de Toni, *Le piante e gli animali in Leonardo da Vinci.* Bologna (1922).

(106) A. Baldacci, *Le piante e la pittura di Leonardo da Vinci.* Bologna 1930

(107) Arturo Farinelli, *Sentimento e concetto della natura in L. da V.,* in *Miscellanea di studi critici ed. in onore di Arturo Graf.* Bergamo 1903.

(108) O. Münsterberg, *Leonardo und die chinesische Landschaftsmalerei,* in *Orientalisches Archiv,* 1911.

(109) Francesco Malaguzzi Valeri, *La Corte di Ludovico il M. o.* Milan 1915 (vol. II, Bramante e Leonardo).

(110) Emil Möller, *Salai und Leonardo da Vinci* in *Jahrbuch d. Kunsthist. Samml. in Wien.* Vienna 1928, pp. 139-161.

(111) J. Strzygowski, *Leonardo, Bramante, Vignola im Rahmen vergleichender Kunstforschung,* in *Mitteilungen d. Kunsthist. Inst. zu Florenz,* III, 1919.

LEONARDO THE SCULPTOR

(112) L. Courajod, *Léonard de Vinci et la statue équestre de Francesco Sforza.* Paris 1879.

(113) Fr. Haak, *Zur Entwicklung des italienischen Reiterdenkmals,* in *Zeitschr. f. bild. Kunst,* N.F. VII, 1896, p. 273 et seq.

(114) Simon Meller, *Die Reiterdarstellungen Leonardos und die Budapester Bronzestatuette,* in *Jahrb. d. preuss. Kuntsamml.,* Berlin 1916, pp. 113-140.

(115) A. Cook, *The Signa Madonna.* London 1919.

(116) A. Cook, *Leonardo da Vinci, Sculptor.* London 1923. (See the review by Sir Eric Maclagan, in Burlington Magazine XLIII, 1923, II, p. 69 et seq.)

(117) Francesco Malaguzzi Valeri, *Leonardo da Vinci e la scultura.* Bologna 1922.

(118) Franz Landsberger, *Die künstlerischen Probleme der Renaissanc.* Halle 1922 (p. 72 et seq. Equestrian monuments).

(119) Raymond S. Stites, *Leonardo da Vinci, Sculptor,* in *Art Stud* 1926 (p. 103 et seq.) 1930 (p. 254 et seq.), 1931 (p. 289 et s. Cambridge, U.S.A.

See also Nos. 57 and 63.—Bode (in No. 79) developed str ideas about Leonardo as a sculptor; on this subject he neve. better than in his article in the *Jahrbuch d. preuss. Kunstsamml.* X. 1904, p. 125 et seq., "Leonardo als Bildhauer" (reprinted in first edition of "*Florentiner Bildhauer*", pp. 286-302).

THE ENGRAVINGS OF THE SCHOOL OF LEONARDC

(120) Adam Bartsch, *Le Peintre-Graveur,* vol. XIII, p. 83, 331. Vienna 1811.

(121) J. D. Passavant, *Le Peintre-Graveur,* Vol. V, pp. 179-184. Leipzig 1864.

(122) G. d'Adda, *Léonard de Vinci, la gravure milanaise et Passavant.* Paris 1868.

(123) A. Blum, *Léonard de Vinci, Graveur,* in *Gazette des Beaux Arts,* II, 1932, p. 88 (with bibliography).

INDEX TO BIBLIOGRAPHY